SHATTERED VOWS

SHATTERED VOWS

Priests Who Leave

David Rice

William Morrow and Company, Inc.
New York

This book is based on original interviews; however, some names have been changed to protect the privacy of certain individuals.

Library of Congress Cataloging-in-Publication Data

Rice, David, 1945–
    Shattered vows : priests who leave / David Rice.
      p.   cm.
    Includes bibliographical references and index.
    ISBN 0-688-07805-2
    1. Ex-priests, Catholic. 2. Catholic Church—Clergy. 3. Catholic Church—
Discipline. I. Title.
    BX4868.2.R52   1990
    262'.142—dc20   90-39287
                                            CIP

Printed in the United States of America

First Edition

1 2 3 4 5 6 7 8 9 10

BOOK DESIGN BY A. DEMAIO

To
Luci

CONTENTS

PROLOGUE
"Remember Me"

I will judge no man until I have walked in his moccasins for six months.

Native American proverb

FOR nine years Don Franco Trombotto, forty-five years old, had been the parish priest of Vilaretto, one of those Italian alpine villages that comes alive in summer for the tourists and drowses all winter under its blanket of snow. On January 26, 1985, Don Trombotto hanged himself in the corridor of his parish house, just outside his bedroom door.

"We arrived and cut him down and put him on his bed," the brigadier of the regional *carabinieri* said.

On the kitchen table were three letters. The first contained telephone numbers to be called immediately. The second contained the priest's will. The third contained his farewells and some thoughts on his life. "In my last hour," Franco Trombotto had written, "here in the silence of my room, while snow is falling outside, I ask Jesus Christ to be my savior. I say to him the prayer of the Good Thief—remember me. I have carried my cross a long way: now I fall under the cross."

The letter made no reference to Don Trombotto's twenty-year-long love for a local woman. However, a priest friend, Don Franco Barbero, wrote to the press about it, angered at Church attempts to cover up the suicide as a sudden illness. He wrote bluntly that his friend had been in love for twenty years, but in the end, not being able to make it official, had killed himself. "He had asked me," Barbero said, "if people were talking about him, if I had heard anything. He feared above all that his mother might know he had left orthodoxy."

The local paper[1] stressed the utter loneliness of the dead man. For nine years he had tried to break through to his parishioners, learning their Piedmontese dialect, but to no avail. The long winter evenings were for him an obsession. "They only look to me for baptisms and funerals," Don Trombotto had once said. The paper said that solitude is the condition of many priests in the Alps. "Long ago people used to confide in their priests; they were invited from house to house. But today, even in the country, priests play a marginal role. The TV is the *padrone* in every home: Pippo Baudo [a TV character] rules the Sunday."

In his loneliness Don Trombotto had looked for love. "He felt," continued the paper, "that if he followed that love, canon law would have deprived him of his priesthood." This he could not have borne. "He wanted to live in fullness *and* in the priesthood," Barbero wrote. He could not, and he died.

The dead priest's letter asked pardon for the trouble to his bishop and his parents. And his last thought was for the boys with whom he went climbing in the summer. "Be more friendly and generous with your priest," he wrote. "And do not leave him alone at the altar."

Suicides of priests are not confined to the lonely alpine valleys of Italy. I have come across a considerable number of these suicides—in one instance, four in one city—in places as far apart as the United States and Ireland, and one priest who killed himself I knew very well. Within the last three days, as I am writing this manuscript, I have heard of two further suicides.

It is the most final way of all to leave the priesthood of the Roman Catholic Church (or rather, to leave the formal ministry, for one is a priest forever). Yet it is but a symptom of one of the most grievous crises to have hit that church since the Reformation. Hardly more than two decades after the Vatican Council, Pope John's dream of a Church renewed has shattered into one hundred thousand pieces, each of those pieces a priest who left his ministry, which is almost a quarter of all the active priests in the world.

Those one hundred thousand shepherds did not shuffle out into the mist with downcast heads. Most of them marched resolutely out, vowing to take no more; others stormed out in fury and disgust; many simply got up from their knees, made the sign of the cross, and walked quietly away. The rate could be calculated at more than one every two hours, for more than twenty years, they left . . . and left and left. And still they leave: Right now, according to sociologist Richard Schoenherr, 42 percent of all American priests leave within twenty-five years of ordination.[2] That means that by now half of all American priests under sixty have left.

Already over two fifths of the parishes in the world have no resident priest,[3] and by the turn of the century the number will be half. "The hungry sheep look up, and are not fed," as Milton said.

The conventional wisdom about priests' leaving is that the good priests stay and the bad ones leave. Or, if not the bad ones, at least the weaklings, the cowards, the selfish ones. But it is not quite that simple. Sometimes it is even hard to decide who really stayed and who left. What of a priest who marries with the Church's blessing and continues working in a Rio de Janeiro slum at his bishop's request? Has he left? What of the priest who really wants to leave but elects to stay inside the structure because he might not survive outside it and settles for a life centered on himself? Has he not left, even if it is only "inner emigration"? What of a priest who is still "celibate" and insists that celibacy excludes only marriage, not sex? Has he left anything?

Left what, anyway? The Church? Very few leave the Church. The priesthood? "Thou art a priest forever." The ministry? I know hundreds who have "left" and have never stopped ministering in many different ways, and in many new ways.

And what about why they leave? Few in the Church dare to ask why is this immense mutiny. It is the Unmentionable Topic. Is it the system? Is it anger at authority? Is it church structures that are unacceptable? Is it celibacy? Celibacy was excluded from discussion at the Vatican Council at the express wish of Pope Paul VI, in a papal letter read to the council on October 11, 1965.[4] Again in 1971 the Synod of Bishops turned down a proposal that called for a married priesthood.[5]

Sociologists have given us clear statistics. We need now to see the human lives they represent: We need to hang flesh on those statistical bones. We need to hear these men speak from the heart, and to hear their wives and children.

In Brazil, Cardinal Aloisio Lorscheider stated clearly what was needed: "I would like more concrete information on the priests who left," he told me. "The reasons why they left. Their situation now. Are they living in anguish or in anger? If we could just see these priests and hear them more profoundly, and perhaps arrive at another solution to the one that exists today. There should be more exchange and dialogue. Because many of these priests were very faithful servants in the ministry, very dedicated. They suffered in coming to their decision to marry, and all of this should be examined more. I think it is a human and a Christian problem that is not being treated as profoundly as it should be."

This book tries to do what Cardinal Lorscheider suggests. In the last several years I have traveled thirty-eight thousand miles to meet and interview priests who left, their wives, and their children. In many parts of the world—throughout the United States, Britain, Ireland, Sicily, Italy, Holland, Germany, France, Spain, Peru, Brazil, Chile, and Colombia*—I have lived with these families, dandled their little ones on my knee, gone for ice cream with the teenagers, sat for hours with the wives and heard their views on this crazy but still-loved Church that is ourselves. I have stayed up into the wee hours with men who were once monsignors and even bishops, and watched their eyes, once opaque and cautious, now sparkle with candor and the sheer joy of life, or flash with unhealed anger, or weep over a grief they had not allowed to surface until we talked.

In the course of my travels I met a total of 442 priests who had resigned from the ministry or married, and talked to 247 of them, alone and in groups. I also spoke with 177 of the wives and women friends of these men, and likewise interviewed 41 of their children.

I also stayed with over one hundred priests still in active ministry, living in anything from parish houses on southern Italy to mission stations in Peru, Brazil, and Chile. Some of those active priests are among the most dedicated and downright good people I have ever met. And some are in pain. But many said, like Cardinal

---

* During the course of my research, I also interviewed married and resigned priests from the following other countries: Argentina, Australia, Austria, Belgium, Bolivia, Canada, Czechoslovakia, Guatemala, Mexico, Honduras, India, Japan, New Guinea, Nicaragua, the Philippines, Poland, Portugal, South Africa, and Zaire.

Lorscheider, go, find out what is happening, and tell us. For all is not well in the Roman Catholic Church.

This book, based on over 530 interviews, as well as on a considerable amount of written sources, turns out to be partly a story of anguish—the anguish that today runs from top to bottom in the Church. The anguish of a frail Pope Paul VI, crying out in 1967 against priests who are "crucifying the Church," choking on words like "Judas." The anguish of Pope John Paul II, his arms outstretched, pleading that "we do not return the gift once given,"[6] and cutting off all dispensations to leave the ministry.

There is the anguish of indecision before a man leaves, and sometimes afterward the anguish of guilt, laced with hunger and poverty and rejection by churchmen. There is the anguish of the spouse, branded as Eve the Temptress; there is the shame of families and the heartbreak of mothers; there is the hurt and loneliness of fellow priests who choose to stay.

Anguish is, however, far from the whole story. Rather it is akin to the pain before birth. For I found on my voyages that something splendid is gestating inside the Catholic Church. I may have been inside more married priests' homes than perhaps anyone else in the world has, and I feel gratitude for the hope and joy I found there.

This book will try to explore this hope in the hearts and hearths of the priests who leave the active formal ministry. It is not a book of statistics but of human probing. To learn of hope, you ask people to open their hearts, often in the quiet of the night.

The reader should be aware of the distinction between secular priests and priests of a religious order. Roughly speaking, secular priests belong to a local diocese and are under the direct authority of the bishop of that diocese. They usually live alone, or with one or two others in rectories. They do not make vows, but Church law requires that they be celibate—that is, that they do not marry. Priests, however, who belong to religious orders, take vows of poverty, chastity, and obedience, and normally live in a community based on the tradition of the monasteries. These priests are often called "religious." If celibacy eventually becomes optional for priests, it could come about that the secular priests would be free to marry, and that religious orders, with their community traditions, would be the natural and supportive environment for those who choose celibacy.

CHAPTER 1

The Shattering

The Devil's mirror fell and shattered into hundreds of millions of pieces. . . . Two splinters from the mirror hit little Kai—one entered his heart and the other his eyes. Poor Kai, soon his heart would turn to ice, and his eyes would see nothing but faults in everything.
Hans Christian Andersen, "The Snow Queen"

In October 1968 the Archdiocese of San Antonio, Texas, erupted. It was an eruption of fury and frustration and recrimination the likes of which had not been seen before in the American Catholic Church. It began when local priests demanded that the pope fire their archbishop and got fired themselves instead.

The aftershocks of that eruption are still being felt in San Antonio. I have watched men fall silent as they tried to recount for me those events of two decades ago, and have seen tears run down their cheeks. I have heard others, still raw with anger, utter words of hatred I was amazed to hear from them. I have also met men whose lives are dedicated to healing the wounds of that awful year.

The story of San Antonio is relevant today, not just because the wounds still bleed, but because the Texas of two decades ago is a microcosm of the worldwide Roman Catholic Church today.

* * *

It was the best of times; it was the worst of times. The best because those days after the Vatican Council shimmered with energy and hope for spring in the Roman Catholic Church. The worst because the powerful leader of the Archdiocese of San Antonio grew progressively more autocratic.

For most of his life, Archbishop Robert Emmet Lucey had spoken out fearlessly for the underdog and was a tireless champion of trade unions. Except, that is, for the clergy of his own diocese. A champion of liberty for others, he was a ferocious authoritarian toward his own priests. They accepted it for years, and went out and fought his battles, and gladly preached his doctrine of civil and personal rights, because they believed in it. But they learned it too well. "Lucey created a monster out of us," says Ray Henke, at that time the spiritual director at the local seminary. "He took us Texan farm boys and radicalized us in social justice. But then when these priests wanted to apply workplace democracy in the Church, Lucey could not handle it."

Lucey came back from the Second Vatican Council a changed man, which was attributed to his having been frightened by all the talk of collegiality. When his own priests began to organize into an association, just as the council had told them to, he could not deal with it. He was growing old, and like an aging lion seeing the pride drift away, he grew dangerous. And cruel. "When they come after me," he was heard to say, "they'll come to kill me."

Much of the blame for what subsequently happened was pinned on the archbishop's right-hand man, Monsignor Leroy Manning, who was both chancellor and vicar-general of the diocese for twenty-eight years. Even today the hatred expressed for him is astonishing. "If murder wasn't against the law, I'd have to stand in line to do him in," one resigned priest told me. "The guy seemed to take a particular delight in disciplining people. I frequently said, and I mean it literally, that if he ever met a violent end, I'd feel sad because I had nothing to do with it. Quite frankly, the only reason he's alive at all is that it would not be worth going to jail to do him in."

In those years after the council, things in the San Antonio archdiocese got worse and worse, until, as Fr. Joe Till says, "you could smell the fear." Priests seen as ringleaders were sent to rehab homes for alcoholic priests. Many others were assigned and reassigned, over and over again, in a way that was clearly intended to punish them. As one local priest pointed out to me, "Even the

military knows you just don't keep moving people around anymore.'' To transfer people without any reference to where their
social contacts are, especially when they are celibate and have no
families or loved ones to go with them, was, he believes, ''tantamount to a breach of their civil rights.''

''A young man would be moved four times in the space of nine
months, just like a pawn,'' Fr. Joe Till recalls. ''After a while he
wakes up one day, looks at himself in the mirror, and says, 'Maybe
there's something wrong with me.' As a result, guys had nervous
breakdowns.'' Another priest recalls the diocese's refusing to pay
psychiatrist's fees for a man who had had a breakdown. ''There was
a sense of doom and gloom that was palpable. There was fear,
uncertainty. Guys would go into a tizzy if the phone rang. If they
heard the chancery office wanted to see them, they'd go bananas
almost. It was intimidation.''

There was one old alcoholic priest called in to the chancery
office (where the diocese is administered). ''He was an alky, no
doubt about it,'' another priest remembers. ''They call him in, they
tell him he's a no-good alky. 'You are suspended, removed, get out
of the diocese in twenty-four hours. We don't care where you go.'
Maybe they just want to scare him. Well, he goes home, puts a
shotgun to his mouth, and blows his head off.''

''It was an era in the diocese when justice without love was the
order of the day,'' Monsignor Balty Janacek says. At one point, a
book by the Jesuit John L. McKenzie, saying that authority should
be exercised in a spirit of love,[1] was discussed at the priest's senate.
The archbishop was furious, saw it as an attack on himself, and
denounced the book as heretical.

At a secret meeting in the basement of St. Anne's Church,
thirty priests got together to form a priests' association. Lucey's
spies were there and told him. Then came the recriminations—
picking off the leaders, firing them out of their parishes, and sending
them to the Texas boondocks.

Jim Brandes, the head of Catholic Charities in the archdiocese,
called it witch-hunting and was reported. He was summarily fired
and told to report as assistant pastor in Victoria, Texas. ''He was the
first who refused to go,'' recalls Roy Rihn, now a pastor in the
diocese. ''He was the first one to say, fuck it, I ain't gonna go.[2] Jim
was a strong guy, but he just crumbled. Well, I was president of the
priests' association. And what happened to Brandes really got to

me. I got depressed, seeing this fine man destroyed. Emotions were running very high.''

Shortly afterward, the men on the seminary faculty took a working weekend at a house on nearby LBJ Lake. While they were there, a phone call notified them of two more transfers. Roy Rihn remembers "spending a sleepless night. We've got to do something, I thought. This can't go on. So the next morning I announced, 'Fellas, I couldn't sleep last night: I can't live with myself and see people destroyed. We have to do something.' What we didn't know, of course, was that one of the people there was reporting to the bishop.''

The upshot was that the priests' association prepared a letter to Pope Paul VI asking for Lucey's resignation. The letter was signed by fifty-one priests on September 16, and later by another seventeen. Four signers were from the seminary faculty. "There is an atmosphere of fear, alienation and dissatisfaction on the part of many priests in this archdiocese,'' the letter told the pope. "We are like camels crossing an increasingly arid desert, upon whose back there has just been placed the proverbial last straw.'' The atmosphere was being made tenser by "a long line of vindictive and repressive transfers'' of priests, and by Lucey's "aloofness, repression and paternalism.'' The priests asked for a fact-finding commission to be sent by Rome, and requested a say in the naming of the next archbishop.

The letter was to stay secret, with copies only to Archbishop Lucey, to the Vatican's representative in Washington, and to a couple of other key people. But it ended in a warning: "We want you to know that we are so determined that if we shall not have received within 30 days some positive sign of action on our requests, we will make this letter public to the news media, and we will involve the Catholic laity in our appeal.''[3]

Roy Rihn now thinks the ultimatum was a mistake. Lucey's comment was: "You don't give ultimatums to the Holy Father.''

Under the cool crust of the archdiocese the magma was seething. Lucey himself passed copies of the letter to his loyal priests and laymen, telling them to get ready for a fight "if the rebels publish their garbage.'' He asked the Vatican for "a canonical trial for the conspirators.'' His principal targets were Rihn and the seminary men.

At the seminary they still remember "Black Monday,'' the morning Archbishop Lucey arrived with eight officials and ordered the students to appear one by one before an inquisition on seminary discipline and the behavior of the faculty. The students came close to rioting, and the rector had to intervene to stop the proceedings.

That month was like the time of the Phony War with all its feints and maneuverings. The day after Black Monday, Lucey sent a message to the rebels through one of his priests. "Tell them I have asked the Holy Father to send a neutral observer into the diocese," Lucey said. This was the long-awaited sign from the Vatican, but tragically no one realized it. Roy Rihn still grieves over their mistake. "We just didn't recognize the niceties of Vatican protocol," he says. "We thought the archbishop was trying to delay things. I've learned since that the pope, through the apostolic delegate in Washington, ordered Lucey to do this. But at the time, not a single one of us recognized this as the sign."

So they rejected the overture and called the fateful news conference at the Menger Hotel. Fr. Charlie Hersig read out the letter and a prepared statement that filled in the background for press and television, stressing that the action "does not destroy, nor does it intend to deny, the authority of the Church." And all of a sudden the San Antonio affair became national news. The diocese split from end to bitter end, with laity and priests marching on the archbishop's house and others rallying to support the beleaguered church officials.

Nine days later, the four key members of the seminary staff— the rector, vice rector, dean of men, and spiritual director—were ordered to report to the archbishop at five-minute intervals, starting at 10:30 A.M. It was like the timetable for a hanging. They entered the archbishop's sanctum one by one, to be told that they were removed from office, that they were not even to return to the seminary. They were not being given alternative assignments, but were to report to Padua Place, a nursing home for elderly priests as well those with difficulties.

The four, Roy Rihn, Ray Henke, Louis Michalski, and Bob Walden, decided they would not go. Without a penny of income, they rented a house in a poor barrio on the city's west side. Soon Henke and Walden got jobs and helped support the others, and Rihn, the onetime seminary rector, became sort of housemother to everyone. Gifts poured in from laypeople. Gradually it became known as "the House on Pinto Street," and for a long time it was a kind of halfway house for any priest in trouble in San Antonio.

The firings and the reassignments continued. After months of waiting, the rector of the other (preparatory) seminary was suddenly summoned, called a traitor, and fired. Lucey himself had planned to resign a couple of days later, which in fact he did. Within a year, over thirty priests of the San Antonio diocese had left the ministry, and the exodus continued long after Lucey's retirement.

In the midst of all the stress, Fr. Joe Novak collapsed and died from a heart attack, the day after a confrontation with Lucey. At the funeral mass, Lucey preached on the Five Foolish Virgins.

Roy Rihn continued the housekeeping in Pinto Street, ''until it became clear to me my brothers had each found kind women to share their pain. It was obvious our arrangement was not going to last much longer. I became depressed. Then I got an offer to be the campus chaplain up in Oklahoma. I asked the archbishop, and he refused. I hit the skids and had to be hospitalized for depression. The doctor wrote to Lucey: 'Either you let him go, or it'll be on your head.' So he let me go. It saved my life.''

Today Monsignor Roy Rihn is a well-loved pastor in San Antonio. Ray Henke is married and a respected psychotherapist in the city. Louis Michalski and Bob Walden are also married. Joe Till and Balty Janasek have stayed active priests. Of those who signed the letter, at least twenty-four later married, some waiting several years before leaving. Many live around San Antonio today; some have died; a couple have disappeared. Charlie Hersig is the bishop of Tyler, Texas; Edmondo Rodriques is a Jesuit provincial. Larry Steuben is the personal assistant to the present archbishop.

In the years that followed, other priests who had never signed left the ministry to marry. The diocese, which in 1967 had 441 priests, has 386 today.[4] Archbishop Lucey died in retirement in 1977. To his dying day he referred to the events of 1968 as ''the Massacre.'' Others called it ''the Alamo.'' His chancellor, Leroy Manning, at seventy-three is the pastor of Boerne, Texas, where he keeps a loaded revolver on a table beside the front door.

Nearly twenty bitter years passed. Some of the priests who left and married had formed Connections, a small association for themselves and their wives. Gentle Roy Rihn, ever the brother and bridge builder, kept in touch, even conducted prayer weekends for the married priests and families. A new kind of archbishop reigned in San Antonio—Mexican-American Patrick Flores. They call him the Mariachi Bishop.

Then came the little miracle of MO ranch. One day Roy Rihn was having coffee with his old married buddy Ray Henke. He happened to mention that the San Antonio priests were getting together for a weekend of prayer and discussion at a retreat center called MO Ranch.

"Some of us should come," said Henke. "We're priests too!"

Rihn laughed. Then he said, "Seriously, Ray, would you like to come? How about I put it to Flores—that some of our married brothers would like to join us?"

So finally, married priests Ray Henke and John Orr were invited to come for the Friday evening and stay overnight. When they arrived, thoroughly nervous, they were told, you guys are on at 7:00 P.M. They were brought in to the assembled priests and got a standing ovation. "It was electrifying," a priest told me. "It brought tears to many eyes."

Ray Henke spoke first. "When I left, I was hurt by many of you," he told the priests. "But I also know my leaving hurt very many of you. For this I am sorry."

One youngish priest got up and said, "Ray, you really did hurt me when you left. I looked up to you. I admired you so very much—I looked forward to spending my priesthood side by side with you. When you left, my world collapsed."

Ray just said, "I'm sorry." And the two of them came together and embraced. That was the turning point. Others began to ask pardon. It was a reconciliation process that went on way past midnight.

The next morning, Archbishop Flores spoke at the mass. "I am ashamed," he said, "that we had to wait for our married brothers to come to us for reconciliation. We should have gone to them." He said he had just returned from Cuba where he had met Castro. If we can do that with a Communist leader, Flores pointed out, why not with our brothers who are no longer active in the ministry? He pledged that it would be a priority of his administration to bring these men, and their wives and families, back into using their talents in whatever way possible in the Church.

The group then established a Resigned and Active Priests' Committee, which the following March held Bridging the Years, a reconciliation retreat where over eighty resigned and active priests shared hurts and memories. It was a beautiful day, a priest told me, with a lot of healing. Since, there have followed gatherings of whole families with the active priests, including Christmas parties at the archbishop's house.

But it was only a start, and now the euphoria has faded, there is a sense of anticlimax. For some priests, whether active or resigned, it's maybe enough to have buried the hatchet. Others, though, would like to see moves to reintegrate married priests in the ministry. However, with Rome's present stance, they can go no further. One pastor, after MO Ranch, invited the married priest Louis Fritz and his wife, Rosemary, to do a weekly communion service in a chapel that had no priest. It was very successful until some other Texas bishops got word of it and intervened with Archbishop Flores. Fritz had to quit.

As Ray Henke puts it, it's a bit like ecumenism. Once the hand shaking is over, where can you really go?

And tragically, there are some, both resigned and active, who have never been reconciled. "They went their way, we went ours," one active priest says. "We have nothing to say to each other."

Hatred and anger still claim their place in San Antonio, and much is still directed at Leroy Manning, Lucey's right-hand man during the cruel years.

I went to see Monsignor Manning in his little parish house in Boerne, Texas. His hair is iron-gray now, and he looks his seventy-three years. In the twenty-nine years he worked for Lucey, he had never liked him, Manning told me. "But, boy, did I respect him. And I was loyal to him. People saw me as his hatchet man, which didn't make me too popular. But it didn't matter as long as they respected me too."

What about reconciliation with the priests who left?

"I've seen very little of them," Manning said. "It would hurt them to see me. It would hurt me to see them. I've been invited to many meetings, but, no, it would hurt too much. It would open those wounds again. There was a meeting recently; had I known about it, I would have purposefully avoided it."

Manning is sad there are so few priests today, but he thinks maybe God is teaching people to be less dependent on the Church. "Maybe God said, 'I'll let y'all see how it feels to be without schools and nuns and priests. The Church has been in worse positions before—you can't kill it.' "

As we parted he embraced me and said, *"Vaya con Dios"*

("Go with God"). And then he called after me from the door, *"Oremus pro invicem"* ("Let us pray for each other").

With hindsight the San Antonio story can be seen as part of one of the most turbulent years of the century: the year of the assassinations of Martin Luther King and of Robert Kennedy; the year of the start of Northern Ireland's troubles; the year of the Tet offensive that turned the Vietnam War around in the United States; the year of student riots in Paris, Mexico City, and Tokyo; the year of the invasion of Czechoslovakia; the year Cardinal Patrick O'Boyle suspended forty-four priests in Washington, D.C. for refusing to go along with the birth control encyclical—in an uproar rivaling San Antonio's in its intensity and anger.

It is not just history. The San Antonio story will not be ended until reconciliation is complete, until those priests hungering for ministry can find it, and those parishes hungering for priests can have them.

But far more significant are the thousands of mini San Antonios that are still happening throughout the Catholic Church every day. They can be as tiny as one man confronting his bishop, or as hidden as one man confronting his own loneliness. And Vatican treatment of its troubled priests today appears no less harsh than San Antonio's treatment twenty years ago. But the present exodus of priests, combined with the desperate lack of vocations, represents a crisis that is without parallel, an enormity that no official secrecy or fear of scandal can bury. It is a crisis that will lead to a Church without priests and thus without the Eucharist.

Professor Richard Schoenherr, a sociologist at the University of Wisconsin at Madison, presents some daunting figures for the United States: "By the tenth anniversary after ordination, on the average, 20 percent of the priests have resigned from the active ministry. By their fifteenth anniversary, an additional 15 percent resign. So that by the time they reach their twenty-fifth anniversary, 42 percent of each ordination class has resigned from the active ministry. . . . In three or four years there are going to be more resigned priests alive in the United States than active priests."[5]

By the turn of the century, the number of priests in the United States will be halved. What it means is this: In 1925 there were fifteen thousand secular priests for sixteen million Catholics; although there are thirty thousand priests today, by the end of the century the number of priests will have dropped back to fifteen thousand, but there will be sixty-five million Catholics for them to serve.[6] And priests in religious orders cannot make up the deficit: Studies show their rate of resignation is even worse.[7]

The consequences for the Church are appalling. The average age of a diocesan priest in the United States today is fifty-seven. By the year 2000 it will be sixty-five. That's retirement age. Already 1,950 U.S. parishes have no priest, and the number keeps growing.[8]

Stress is taking a terrible toll on active priests: The number who die before retirement (at sixty-five) has doubled in recent years. In 1985, according to a study commissioned by the U.S. bishops, 40 percent of U.S. priests reported having "severe personal, behavioral or mental problems in the previous 12 months."[9]

Vocations, the other side of the coin, are also down—from 48,000 seminarians in 1965 to 10,300 today.[10]

Other countries fare no better. One diocese in Spain had one thousand two hundred priests in 1965; it now has two hundred. That is one single diocese losing one thousand priests in two decades. In another diocese, 70 percent of the active parish priests are over fifty-five.[11] Spain has seven thousand priests who have left the ministry, leaving a total of twenty-eight thousand priests still active in the country.

Figaro says the French clergy are facing the greatest crisis of their history. From forty thousand diocesan priests in 1969, there will be fewer than twenty-five thousand in the year 2000.[12]

France has over 5,000 resigned priests.[13] Italy has 8,000.[14] Holland has 2,114.[15] Ireland's bishops admit to 488 who left the ministry through "a definitive act" such as marriage, and the real total is thought to be considerably higher.[16] In Brazil the organization Rumos lists 2,200 resigned priests and estimates there are 1,000 more.[17]

Figures for Britain are almost impossible to get, as no statistics are published on priests' resigning. From the *Catholic Directory* one can glean that, between 1968 and 1987, the number of priests in Britain dropped by 1,526 (from 4,962 secular priests and 2,788 order priests in 1968, to 4,276 secular priests and 1,948 order priests in 1987). During this period the estimated Catholic population rose from 4,143,854 to 4,164,040. However, these gloomy statistics are not even accurate: The 1989 edition of the directory merely repeats the 1987 figures, which had already appeared in the 1988 directory.[18]

The total number of resigned priests throughout the world could be as high as one hundred thousand, the figure generally accepted by the media, and is certainly above eighty thousand. The Vatican's own *Annuarium Statisticum Ecclesiae* lists the granting of 46,302 dispensations to priests to marry, between 1963 and 1983.[19] That was seven years ago. According to research done by the Corpus organization, for every priest who gets a dispensation, there is another who was refused or never bothered to ask. So a figure of one hundred thousand is likely.[20]

Jesuit professor Jan Kerkhofs has compared the number of ordinations each year with the combined totals of deaths and resignations for that year. He has done it for twenty-four countries. For every one hundred priests resigned or died, Holland had eight replacements, Belgium fifteen, Germany thirty-four, France seventeen, Italy fifty, Ireland forty-five, Spain thirty-five, and Portugal ten.[21]

Official church bulletins sometimes suggest that things are better in the third world. They are not. According to Kerkhofs, the extra bodies in third world seminaries are far outweighed by the decline in foreign missionaries and the vast increase in Catholic populations. In one Ugandan diocese, there used to be six thousand Catholics to every priest a few years ago. Ten years later there were thirteen thousand. In Indonesia in 1954, there were eleven priests for every ten thousand people. Two decades later there were only five priests serving that same number.[22]

In the whole world there were 368,000 Catholic parishes and mission stations in 1985. Of these, 157,000 did not have a priest.[23] That's nearly half. For millions upon millions of people that means no mass, no Eucharist, the center of their religion.

The priesthood of the Catholic Church is in deep trouble. As Jesuit John A. Coleman puts it: "Any profession for which the following facts are true—declining absolute numbers in the face of growth of the larger population, significant resignations, a declining pool of new recruits and an aging population—can be referred to as having a deep-seated identity crisis, whatever the internal morale of the group."[24] The Catholic Church has in fact become one huge San Antonio, with many dioceses throughout the world losing a far higher proportion of their priests than ever San Antonio did. Whether all priests leave for similar reasons, the following chapter will examine.

CHAPTER 2

The Scattering

It is not good that man should be alone.
Genesis 2:18

"IN the middle of life's journey I found myself in a dark forest, and could not find my way." In the last two decades those opening words of the *Divine Comedy* came fearfully true for thousands upon thousands of Roman Catholic priests, so that they scarcely knew if paradise or hell lay ahead of them. With purgatory they became thoroughly familiar, a purgatory of greater anguish than Dante had ever conceived.

Some are still suffering. Others have emerged from their purgatory and are fulfilled and active priests. Close to one hundred thousand simply left—that is, they resigned from formal ministry. It is a figure that expresses one of the most extraordinary religious phenomena since the Reformation, a phenomenon as yet unexplained. The men who left—can they explain it? What were their reasons for leaving? I have put that question to hundreds of them around the world.

"Who is the woman?" Thus began a letter from Belgian Cardinal Godfried Danneels to a missionary friend who was leaving in Brazil. Danneels could not have been further from the mark, that friend, Eduardo Hoornaert, told me. Yet *cherchez la femme* is everyone's presumption when a priest leaves. A pious Irish mother put it succinctly when her missionary son left: "There's some bloody Brazilian bitch at the back of this!"

In fact, leaving the formal ministry is far more complex than that, and I found as many reasons for it as there were men to ask.

The first reason was best expressed by Penny Lernoux, a celebrated writer on Latin America, at an international meeting of priests and nuns at Bogotá: "Religious are beginning to discover that vows lose their meaning unless the community in which they live tries to challenge society's dehumanizing elements."[1]

People don't leave Mother Teresa. They leave, like missionary John Carney in Honduras, after seeing kids crowding around to eat the garbage thrown out by his community. They leave in circumstances like those encountered by missionary Mike Breslin in Paraguay. "There were a quarter of a million in the diocese," he told me. "There were thousands of square miles with unpaved roads. We had one U.S. bishop and half a dozen Franciscans with no Spanish or Guarani. Up to a hundred and thirty degrees heat, in terrible conditions, with no water and no electricity. Infant mortality was so great that there was no time for funerals. We threw a rope from the steeple, people would ring it, and we'd just come out and say a prayer over the little body. That thing rang like the doorbell. It still rings in my dreams."

The hundreds of hamlets saw a priest once every three years. Mike and the others felt they had to train local lay leaders—it was the start of the base community idea. "From all the villages we gathered the leaders together for training: They came to us, we shared their lives. I learned Guarani, and instead of staying at a big American rectory, I moved in with an Indian family."

However, the priests got a visit from the apostolic nuncio, the Vatican representative in the region. "The nuncio got hold of the bishop—'You can't do this,' he told him.

"The bishop called in everybody: 'We'll have to reverse all these things, because the nuncio's against it.' We told the bishop the scheme had gone too far, that the leaders would lose face if we dropped the training now.

"But the bishop called another meeting the next week and put us all on the spot. 'You do what I say, or I'll suspend you,' he told us. [Suspension means that a priest is forbidden to function.] One by one he asked us, 'Will you do it? Will you obey?' Right down the line.

"There were unanimous Nos. Right on the spot he suspended the entire diocese. The entire diocese."

Shortly afterward came a cable from Breslin's parent diocese of Brooklyn. It read, SEND BRESLIN HOME.

Breslin is married now and runs a ceramics shop in Brooklyn. He is also one of the founders of the Nehemiah Project for building houses for America's poor, a project being taken up by Congress, and has helped found a phenomenally successful bilingual public school for 850 mostly black and Hispanic Brooklyn youngsters.

Brazilian Ignacio Campo wanted a more virile church, breaking out of the sacristy, a church where love and dedication to others would be fundamental, "not just looking after yourself and your own soul. I give full value to the sacraments, but only where there is faith and commitment to others. Instead we are making the sacraments into just sentimental helps for most people."

For years before he left the ministry, Campo kept a giant map of the world on the wall behind the altar in his church to remind people that God so loved the world. . . . He had ten chapels, trained lay ministers to preach and do eucharistic services, and was organizing groups to tackle problems in factory and community—this was the time of the military dictatorship. He moved out of the parish house to a single room and began hiding fugitives from the police. There were arguments with Cardinal Rossi and with the local bishop, "because I wanted to give importance to the groups demanding social reform, not to the Legion of Mary."

Campo is married now and is a psychotherapist in São Paulo, where he works mostly with the poor. Some of his patients are sent by the local priests.

Men like Campo usually stay in the ministry as long as they see hope in changing Church structures that need changing. When they feel there's no hope, or sense that they themselves could burn out, they resign from the ministry, but not from the Church. Usually they marry later, remain dedicated Catholics and, free of all official constraints, carry on with whatever ministry is possible to them.

Sometimes these men don't leave but are put out by Church authorities. Such a man is Giovanni Battista Franzoni, who quite literally came down in the world. He moved just a few hundred yards down Rome's Via Ostiense, from the abbey basilica of St.

Paul's Outside-the-Walls to a little community of local people, but it was all the way from an abbot's cross and miter to a layman's sweatshirt and jeans.

From the moment he was elected abbot at the young age of thirty-five, Franzoni was a thorn in the sides of the Church and State in Italy. Real trouble began when in 1970 he wrote a public letter to the Italian president asking him to cancel the annual military parade, saying he was aware of "a growing repugnance to glorifying of armaments, bearers of death, as though they were the nation's glory." Then he was taking the workers' side in industrial disputes, attacking the Vatican's concordat with Italy, "which makes the Church a power, in contrast with what the Gospel says the Church should be." In 1971 he joined with other pastors in Rome to demand that unused church property be handed over for the poor, asking the pope to denounce the city's property speculation.

Abbot Franzoni was fast coming down in the world. He was forced to resign as abbot in 1973; he was suspended from celebrating mass in 1974, after he declared in favor of divorce in that year's referendum. In the 1976 elections he was to be found attacking the Christian Democrats. Then, interpreting Christ's words, "Blessed are the poor." he stated that poverty was not wished by God "but by rulers and oppressors, and that God's disciples are called to confront this anomalous situation."[2]

Shortly after that outburst, Franzoni was "reduced to the lay state." The priest forever was now a layman.

By then Don Franzoni, as everybody still calls him, had moved to his new address just down the street. He and a couple of monks had the abbey's permission to start an experimental community on the Via Ostiense. More than a decade later he is still there, and there has grown up a vibrant neighborhood base community, with its own services for the poor, its own center for celebrating the Eucharist, even its own bookstore. They call it the *Spazio Comune* ("Common Ground").

There are priests who quite simply feel they are in the wrong place. Either they cannot stand the clerical environment in which they feel trapped, and have to get out, or they feel excluded from normal life and want to get back into it. These seem to be two sides of the one coin.

"I felt a sense of incredible domination, of being controlled, waking and sleeping," a now-married priest told me in Ireland. "They controlled me by tying me down to the breviary, by the way they moved me around like a pawn, by censoring everything I wrote for publication, even letters to the paper, by locking me inside a black suit (and in Rome even putting me in skirts and shaving the back of my head), by tying a collar around my neck so that I would not relate to people and they could not relate to me. A railway carriage would fall silent when I entered. I finally felt I couldn't breathe, and to this day I feel physical nausea whenever I see a cassock or a black suit."

A number of priests' wives tell me their husbands have almost a physical revulsion for black and cannot be got to wear it.

I listened to a group of Italian married priests and their wives discussing the wearing of cassocks in the street, which was compulsory until the mid-1960's. *Un usanza pessima* ("a dreadful custom") one of them described it.

"You know what the people called us?" said another priest. "The third sex. They mocked us for wearing skirts. And that's why the Church made us wear them."

"The role of the cassock," one of the priests' wives told me, "was to make the priest feel no longer like a man. A young man who came out of the seminary dressed like that was a stranger among people. He could not fit into daily life. And that's what the Church wanted. These men weren't to have a human personality, but a piloted personality, directed by the canon law. The purpose is to put the priest in a caste apart so that he is apart from everything, especially women." The black suit and Roman collar have the same effect, and they are still required dress in most regions.[3]

While men like these felt oppressed by symbols, others went straight for the oppression they perceived behind the symbols. "I wanted out of a system where there is no term of office, no control, no appeal," a priest in New Jersey said. "And where everything is cloaked under silence. And that's how it is: Bishops are in for life; if they're unjust, there's nowhere to appeal, no higher court, no due process. And half the human race is excluded from all power—I mean the women. It's against the UN Declaration of Human Rights. I believe in the Church, but these are human abuses. It's just ecclesiastical city hall, and I couldn't fight it."

Priests like that one felt locked in. Others felt locked out— from the real world. "I felt I had my nose pressed against the window of other people's lives," one married priest said. "I envied anybody, even gypsies, garbage collectors, the youngsters in the youth club enjoying first love. My heart would tighten up watching them."

Another told me his hand would start shaking as he was giving out communion, "and I just wished I was down at the back of the church, saying my prayers." That man left, and his hands are steady now.

It is interesting that many priests resented their very privileges—the deference, people picking up the check in restaurants for them, the "clerical discount," the gifts of what they call "celibacy vaccine" (liquor). "In New York or Boston you just had to throw your breviary on the front seat of the car, and you never got a parking ticket," a priest told me.

A former missionary in Australia says he just wanted to be like St. Paul the tentmaker. "Just to earn my bread by the sweat of my brow. And after I left, it was such a relief to get that first paycheck. You know," this man said, "I've never been an ordinary person in my life. I came out of school, went into the seminary. I never had the freedom to go out and make a fool of myself. And laypeople don't help when they keep saying, 'You chaps have a great time. You'd never survive outside.' It was something I had to do—prove I could survive."

Some priests leave because they are no longer sure what a priest is, or is supposed to do. Fr. Clete Kiley, the personnel director of the Chicago archdiocese, told me the key question is the identity crisis of priests. With so few priests, many have to be "circuit riders," going from place to place. "Our fear for our priests," Kiley said, "is, do they become sacramental machines? Technically a parish must have a pastor, but the duty person could be a nun or layperson. Which leads to the ID question—what is the priest's role?" Add to this the growing indifference on the part of laypeople, their lack of support for their clergy, and the fact that "our priests are very viciously attacked in the media, mostly by conservative and right-wing elements, and the Vatican seems attentive to these."

My interviews bear this out. Many priests, faced with all this uncertainty and indifference, opt for the warmth and tangible certainties of a job, wife, family, and children.

* * *

Closely linked to this is the motive of loneliness.

I have seen it. While researching this book I stayed with an Italian pastor in a little town in Calabria in southern Italy. Don Antonio is a man of prayer. Each morning he asked me to join him in praying the breviary in the empty church before mass. I accompanied him on his rounds of parishioners and saw the respect with which they received him. The young men all had a smile and a nod for him. But I could almost taste his loneliness. It was in his eyes during morning mass; it was in his face the day he bade me farewell.

Don Antonio lives alone and never cooks for himself, saying fruit and cheese are all he needs. He eats standing at the kitchen table. Off the kitchen is a dining room, pleasantly furnished with a big table and six chairs, suggesting hopes and expectations of years ago. It is never used.

Yet one day I cooked spaghetti carbonara for us both, and Don Antonio ate it with relish. We had some wine that evening, and during the meal I asked him point-blank if he would live his life over the same way.

He shook his head. "No. Not unless they changed the priesthood totally. Only then. Only maybe."

Why he had never married? I asked.

He shrugged. "Maybe I just never found my *grand'amore* ['the love of my life']," he said.

What keeps Don Antonio going? "*Dio solo* ['God alone']. But I never ask him for anything. I just say, 'Thank you, God.' At first, years ago, I begged; I despaired. Now I don't know how to ask anymore."

One evening we sat together in the silence of the presbytery. I was reading a book; he was sorting some papers. A Vespa scooter puttered past in the little street below our window, and it seemed that all joy and life was in that sound. It suddenly struck me that nobody had rung the doorbell that day, and the phone had rung only once. The terrible words of Swinburne went through my mind: "Thou has conquered, O pale Galilean; the world has grown gray from thy breath." Only it's not really the Galilean's fault.

When Don Antonio saw me off at the bus station, I thanked him. "I was happy here with you," I said. I had been. He embraced me and whispered in Latin a line from the Psalms: "How good and sweet it is, for brethren to dwell together in unity."

Pamela Shoup, who married California Jesuit Terry Sweeney,

winner of five Emmy Awards, told me this: "I thought when I first met Terry, this man has more friends than the universe. At lunch one day Terry started to cry. I asked myself, who takes care of this person, who holds him when he cries? Where does he take his fear? When we were first married, Terry took a box out of the back of the closet. It was one of his Emmy Awards, just sitting in there. He was so alone, he hadn't bothered to open it."

Loneliest of all are missionaries and priests who have left their homeland. Few laypeople can grasp how lonely. Sean Connolly describes it in Texas: "Sundays were the worst. You did all the masses. All the baptisms. After mass I'd sit on the wall by the church and chat to the few people going by. I used to envy the local priests—they could go home to Ma on Sunday. I used to sit on that wall outside St. Cecilia's—the intensity and pain of it—feeling, I don't belong to anyone here."

And returning home can be worse. Missionaries in Brazil call it the *amargo ritorno* ("the bitter homecoming"). The space you once had is overgrown, and no one knows what to do with you.

Fr. Tony Conry, still a priest in São Paulo, remembers visiting his Irish hometown and sitting in a pub there.

"Where are you now, Father?" says a young man sitting at the bar, drinking a pint, and watching Gaelic football on the television.

"I'm in Brazil."

"Oh. Well, uh, that must be an interesting place, surely. Hey, Mick, what's the score for Galway now?"

Which brings me to celibacy as the next reason why men leave the ministry. I distinguish celibacy from falling in love, as they are quite different motives for leaving. Celibacy is defined simply as the state of being unmarried. It is not the same as chastity, which means abstaining from genital sexual activity (or confining such activity to the marriage bed if one is married).

Professor Adrian Hastings of Leeds University, England, explained in 1978 why he left the ministry of the Catholic priesthood. He said that for over fifteen years he had not believed in celibacy, yet had lived by it and remained in the ministry, as it gave him a stronger base from which to argue against celibacy. He was not lonely, and loved his priesthood.

However, he changed his mind and decided to marry, partly because he found that the Church heeds deeds more than arguments.

Besides, he said, "I do not believe it to be a just law or a good law, or a law which the Church had the right to make, and I am convinced that it does not express God's will for the Church today, if it ever did. . . . Wherever one turns, the clericalism which puts celibacy above ministry is strangling the Church."[4]

Scores of priests have told me how they were taken into seminaries and set aside for celibacy even before their teens, without a notion of the awesome undertaking it was. And they have spoken of their incredible ignorance and lack of preparation.

Bob Guidry remembers a conversation he had with another ninth grade kid in Houston's junior seminary. Both boys would have been thirteen or fourteen years old and were discussing problems with masturbation.

Bob: "This celibacy thing—dunno how I'm gonna make it. But I guess God'll help me."

Other kid: "Do they cut your balls off?"

Bob: "I dunno. But if they have to do it, I guess they have to do it."

Kids like that sleepwalked into celibacy. Thousands of them awoke in their thirties and beheld with horror the cage they had wandered into. And they simply forced aside the bars and clambered out. Once outside, they started looking for that intimacy they had never had, and that they desired even more than sexual fulfilment.

At the Easter vigil in 1952, a German youngster Heinz-Jürgen Vogels felt a powerful call from God to be a priest: "So absolutely sure was I that this was my vocation that I could not even pray 'Thy Will Be Done,' without being a priest. But that very night, I went around home weeping for hours, not knowing why. In the end I realized it was because from now on I could no longer marry. I had a most tender relationship with a girl in high school. But I knew I would have to renounce everything.

"All during my seminary studies I had this strong and ineffable vocation to priesthood, and the inevitable sensation of incapacity for celibacy. An invincible sadness endured all through those years. But no one said you don't have a vocation. Three months after my ordination I entered a depression, unable physically to move. It took me an hour even to get up out of bed. I thought continually of suicide. I was like an animal playing dead: The soul was aware that the door to marriage was finally closed by ordination. With that door closed, I could not live anymore."

In both Holland and Brazil I have heard priests describe an atmosphere of impending change in the decade of the seventies.

In Holland it followed on the famous Dutch Pastoral Council, that assembly of the Dutch Church that raised so many hopes before it was suppressed by Rome in 1971. The assembly sent Cardinal Alfrink to Rome to ask for optional celibacy. He got nowhere, of course, but because of the Dutch bishops' openness, much seemed possible. In this time of almost Renaissance euphoria, it seemed as if compulsory celibacy would soon go the way of Friday abstinence or fasting from midnight. So some priests decided not to bother waiting. "It was a kind of springtime," Fr. Lambert van Gelder recalls. "And many priests thought, now is the time to marry. I'll go and find me a woman. There were others that already knew a girl. They took the chance and went ahead and married."

A married priest in Brazil describes the sense of expectation there: "At the time, a married priesthood was in the air. Everyone was talking about married men being accepted as community leaders, and being prepared for ordination. All thought it would be the first step. It was tied up with the base community idea—we thought that each community would have a married man looking after it, that would later get ordained."

Cardinal Arns evidently thought so, for he set up a four-year night course to train hundreds of parish leaders, who, everyone hoped, would later be ordained.

A missionary remembers the sense of expectation in São Paulo: "In the early seventies, the feeling was we were coming to the crunch. There would be a decision on celibacy, and a married priesthood was inevitable in Brazil. Well, we were mostly in our thirties: We felt that if you didn't make a move and set things up, you'd be high and dry when the pope said, 'It's all right, boys.'

"They all thought worker priests were coming too. So all the boys went and did training courses at the *Cultura Inglese*, to be teachers. The feeling was, you were going to work, to marry and have a family, and be a priest in a small base community. Of course it was never expressly put in those terms. You could just sense it."

But nothing happened.

"I saw one of the lads when he turned forty. It was a sort of a crisis: He called all his friends for a meal. He said, 'I'm not going to reach fifty without knowing what it's all about.'

"Later we saw him around with a woman.

"Then I guess this pope came in 1978, and it was clear there wasn't going to be any change by anybody. We'd just continue working in a parish. I saw the boys who were still around—perhaps they had waited too long. I felt that one or two of them had their girls—you'd see them with them—but who am I to say? But after that, most of them withdrew from the teaching. They'd given up hope."

Here I should mention what I call the "Whittington factor." In the English legend, young Dick Whittington leaves with his cat for London after an old villager tells him, "Go now, my boy, while you still can. I wanted to go when I was young, but I left it until it was too late."

Many a young priest has heard almost those words. A young Benedictine had almost a father-son relationship with his pastor in northern Minnesota. "We had fun together. He had a hard time getting around to it, but eventually he did tell me, 'You really ought to get out before it's too late.' "

An Irish priest from Sligo remembers working in a parish in Liverpool: "The parish priest was this old guy with egg down his cassock. His main interest was bingo—the principal object in his life. He'd look out at the rain-swept window. 'What a wasted life,' he'd say. 'When I think of my brothers and sisters back home in Ireland, with their families, I wish I had my life all over again.'

"Well, my hair stood on end when I heard him. And I swore there and then, if I'm seventy-five and I think I'm in the wrong thing, I'll quit."

That man did in fact leave and is a teacher now. He is married with three children. His going was hastened when a young priest he knew became a total alcoholic, fell down the stairs, and died from a broken neck.

Vietnam was a factor in leaving the ministry for priests who served as chaplains there. I talked to a number who later married. Tough old Jim Butler of Vista, California, volunteered for two tours as chaplain in Vietnam. He was involved with the Marines in a Combined Action Platoon and was often under fire. These CAPs had among the highest casualty ratings—in one group photo Jim showed me, most of the men had been killed.

"Something happened to me when I was in Nam," Jim told me. "I talked to a couple of doctor friends about it. I guess it was this—I had seen so much death, I wanted to share my life more. I just did not want to go back to rectory life anymore: I could not have taken it.''

Jim met his wife in Arlington Cemetery when he was visiting the graves of his men, and she was visiting her husband's grave.

Charlie Liteky, the only chaplain to win the Congressional Medal of Honor, said almost the same thing on a visit to Dublin. He just needed a spouse. He chose life, after all that death.

Mike McPartland spent his years in Vietnam being dropped out of choppers, with twenty minutes to say mass, and unzipping green bags and anointing whatever he could find inside. ''But the massacre of the innocents on both sides, the death, the destroying and the maiming, I think it sobered a lot of us. All the guys that served there that I knew left the priesthood. I think Nam had tremendous impact on our relationships with God and the diocese—positive with God, negative with the diocese. Every priest walked out of there needing to be loved. As a man, and sexually. Something happened to me: It will never be the same again. I left because I wanted to be loved, and Nam was the catalyst of that. Nam destroyed so many, it's ironic that it made a lot of people whole.''

One priest may leave the ministry for any number of other reasons and later meet a woman and marry her. Another may be struggling with authority or doctrine, suddenly encounter a woman, and leave to marry her. The woman in a case like this could be seen as the occasion on which he leaves, rather than the cause of his leaving. But there are thousands of priests, completely happy with their ministry and with the Church, who quite simply fall in love. And marry. Maryknoll missionary Fr. Dan McLaughlin, himself a lifelong celibate, described it to me with compassion:

''It could well be that a man makes a vow and lives it. And then meets a woman. There is an attraction, but deeper than that, there's a goodness in the person that draws out a goodness in the man. The man says, God wants me to spend my life with her. Do I have a right to deny God's action? I could once have said in all sincerity, I want to make this vow for life. But none of us has power to see down the line. Grace happens not just the day I was born: God acts on us every day of our life. And God could choose to give me the grace to continue in celibacy, or the grace to react to love.''

The love often leads a man to a deeper ministry rather than to a desire to abandon it (even though authority may force him to abandon it). The married priest Everardo Ramirez is a writer in Cartagena, Colombia. He is also a political activist under constant threat of death. He explained to me, from his own experience, how the love of priest and woman can take place in a social context: "In the same barrio where I worked as priest, her family lived. They were great supporters. She and I worked together in the barrio. There began a sympathy which gradually reached a more profound relationship than I have ever had with another woman. The love came in the context of our real work together."

Ramirez recently stood for mayor, representing the left. He lost, and threats against his life have now grown critical. "But," he told me, "my life now is more complete, richer, even though a lot more dangerous. The best of my life, the best of all my books, the best of my effort with gospel and people, has been since my marriage. I have lived with more courage."

Over and over I keep meeting this phenomenon, of love arising in a context of ministry and the couple just wanting to continue their ministry. Brian Eyre of the Irish Holy Ghost Fathers and Marta Almeida of Recife, Brazil, were working together in one of Recife's *favelas*, those massive squatters' slums that teem in every corner of every Latin American city. They organized in the manner of St. Ignatius thirty-day retreats for the local people. He says "The Ignatian retreat is one of the riches of the Catholic Church. But it's not offered to the majority of the poor—it's too long, and it costs money to stay over for thirty days. Well, we broke it up over thirteen weeks and began offering it to the poor. We combined our personalities to give the retreat, and there was a communion of ideas. One day we discovered it was better to continue this journey *caminhada juntos* ['joined together']."

They married, and continued their work for the poor. Brian teaches now to make ends meet.

Priests also leave over doctrinal difficulties, but among the hundreds of resigned priests I have interviewed, the only doctrinal difficulty ever mentioned had to do with *Humanae Vitae,* the papal encyclical forbidding artificial birth control. It must have been some kind of historical watershed: The astonishing thing is that many priests, resigned and active, can remember exactly what they were doing at the moment they heard the news of the encyclical. It's

almost like when Kennedy died—as though, somehow, something
died when that encyclical came out.

"I just don't belong in here," one priest told himself on a
London street one afternoon in 1968. He was looking at an *Evening
Standard* billboard: "Pope Bans Birth Control." It was the day the
Humanae Vitae came out. "My leaving was tipped by the *Humanae
Vitae*," he says now. "That encyclical seemed to say, 'Never mind
what this does to individuals—we must mind the system.' "

Jim Brandes was at breakfast in his Texas rectory when one of
the lay ministers brought in the newspaper announcing the birth
control encyclical. As he remembers it, "The first words out of my
mouth were, 'Oh shit!' It was extraordinarily devastating. All my
abdominal muscles knotted up and stayed that way for weeks. I
actually went for help, professional counseling. And then one day I
was sitting in the rectory, again at the breakfast table, and the words
went through my mind: 'Boy, you have to leave.' Almost immediately my gut relaxed."

Jim Dillon of Tulsa, Oklahoma, was down at his diocesan
mission in Guatemala that fateful year of 1968: "I found there
Indian families with a dozen kids, where it was better that the
weakest would die as an infant than go through life with such
malnutrition. The mission had set up a little health care center and
was introducing the people to the notion of birth control. Then came
the encyclical." And that was that. Everything had to stop.

For Bishop James Shannon, the auxiliary of St.Paul and Minneapolis, and the only Catholic bishop to march with King at Selma,
the encyclical was the last straw that brought him to leave. He
declared he would not keep "two sets of books," privately believing one thing and teaching something else. When he left, he wrote
a letter to the pope: "I cannot in conscience give internal assent,
much less external assent, to the papal teaching in question." Eighteen years later, when I interviewed him in his office as vice president of General Mills in Minneapolis, Shannon had no doubts of
the rightness of his decision.

I myself had a moment of truth some weeks after the encyclical
came out. A young woman came to see me in the Black Abbey,
Kilkenny, Ireland, where I was stationed as a Dominican priest. She
wanted to be told it was all right to use the pill: In those days people
expected the priest to decide for them, and I was silly enough to buy
into that. Her husband, she said, was not bright. "He's awfully

good to me when he gets It—y'know what I mean, Father. But if I refuse him, he beats me up, and then he does it with the dog. And I do get sick, Father.''

Those were her actual words, which I cannot forget.

Since the encyclical she had been saying no to her man and life had become unbearable. Yet deep down, she loved him and wanted to stay with him. So could I let her use the pill, she asked.

I was scrupulous in those days and had felt I must always counsel obedience, although the struggle between obedience and compassion had been tearing me apart. But something snapped in me there and then: For the first time, I did what my gut told me. Go use the pill, I told her. And never mention it to a priest again.

To myself I said, I'll have to face God for my disobedience, but she'll be off the hook. Maybe that's my ministry, to carry God's anger for her and others like her. I remember thinking of Yeats's very first play, *Countess Cathleen*. There is a famine in the land, and all the people have sold their souls to Satan for food. Countess Cathleen offers her own soul in exchange. In the play, of course, Satan accepts the offer because Cathleen's soul is totally good and pure. Unfortunately I couldn't exactly match that!

Such was my thinking in those days. But I was never quite the same from that moment I followed that gut of mine. I think maybe I began to grow up.

The *Humanae Vitae* is one thing. The faith is another. A François Mauriac novel described priests continuing to minister long after they have lost the faith. I can only say that I have never met a man who left the ministry because he lost the faith. I have met several whose faith withered after they left, but that seems to have been tied up with shock and bitterness at the way they were dealt with.

There are priests who burn out, who quietly grind to a standstill after many years of dedicated work. It often happens when there is deep commitment to ministry in very difficult circumstances, combined with the growing realization that Church authorities are either indifferent or hostile.

When I was one of the editors on a paper in Washington State in the 1970s, I sometimes handled stories off the wire about a sixty-year-old chaplain in the strife-torn state penitentiary at Walla Walla. His fight on behalf of the prisoners, and the harassment he suffered from the prison staff, made this priest a sort of hero to me, even though I had never met him.

During the terrible prison takeover of 1979 that lasted 146 days, he became the link to the outside world for inmates confined in often sweltering conditions. Once when he entered a cellblock at the height of the turmoil, the inmates rose to their feet to applaud him. One enormous, burly lifer grabbed his hand: "I never had no use for priests, Father," he said. "But you're an all-right mother!"

Eight years later, when I returned to the Pacific Northwest, it was arranged that I would stay a couple of days in Portland with a married priest called Bob Beh. It was a while before it dawned on me that this big, white-haired, gentle soul, a full colonel in the Army Reserve, with a wife who adored him and whom he deeply loved, was the same man as that Walla Walla chaplain. In November 1981, Beh had resigned as chaplain. After five and a half years in the prison, he had "reached the burnout stage." But the burnout ran deeper than his role as chaplain. Because Bob Beh then resigned as priest, and married.

The Dominican theologian Fr. Liam Walsh said to me recently, "Be sure to point out that while some men remain priests for the wrong reasons, there are some who leave for the wrong reasons." Indeed there are, and I have met a few tragedies. Only God can judge, of course, and those who leave for wrong reasons do not easily confide their motivations. But one gets the impression of a few men who were self-serving in the priesthood and left for what seemed an even more comfortable life outside. Usually it isn't. If such men become successful financially on the outside, they can be distressingly materialistic. If they do not, they can grow very bitter and sometimes pathetic. The only generalization I dare make is that selfish priests seem to become more selfish after they leave.

Then there are some who were neurotic as priests and are neurotic as laymen. Sadly, they too sometimes become more neurotic after leaving. Whether such people left for wrong or right reasons, which of us dare say? It is difficult even to write about many of them, because such people often disappear off the radar screen. But I grieve for them, and I wonder how many there are, and where they are. And I wonder why they are not sought out and cared for by the Church they once served. They should be first among our concerns.

*   *   *

The main reasons why men leave the ministry are not mutually exclusive: Often a man leaves for a cluster of reasons. He may have problems with his bishop and problems with preaching the *Humanae Vitae* at the same time; he may feel the institution is more concerned with medals instead of real ministry; he may be dying of loneliness; he maybe grossly overworked and suffer serious burnout; a good woman may reach in and touch his heart and he may feel that with her he can better minister to others. Or his mother may have just died—many a man has stayed a priest just as long as his mother was alive. There are as many combinations of reasons as there are men out there.

CHAPTER 3
The Sorrowing

For he who lives more lives than one
More deaths than one must die.

Oscar Wilde

FATHER John X came from an Irish country village and was a curate in Dublin, Ireland. He decided to leave the ministry, sending word of this to his family down in the country, but stayed on in the parish for a few weeks until a replacement came. A colleague tells the rest: "A few nights later the priest was set upon outside his presbytery and beaten up most viciously by members of his own family who had traveled to Dublin for that purpose. They were cousins and relatives from the country—presumably they were doing it for God's sake. I remember thinking, such violence comes out of a great fear."

There in a nutshell is gathered all the sorrowing of the priest who leaves: the anguish of the man himself, and the grief, humiliation, and often anger that could drive others to such a pass.

A priest who leaves goes through a particularly fearsome ordeal. It is an ordeal of both fear and loss. There can be fear on the intensity level of someone on death row or in front-line warfare. But whereas the condemned man or the soldier fears for his life, the priest fears for his soul, with a fear carefully nurtured in him since childhood. And whereas the soldier's fear lasts only for those hours or days on the battlefield, the priest's can last for years.

42

There is fear of a world the priest has never lived in, and for which he has been deliberately and expressly unfitted. There is a paralyzing fear of failure and even destitution, that fear the Scripture describes so well: "To dig I am not able, to beg I am ashamed."

There is loss of father, mother, brothers, and sisters, who so often totally reject their loved one when he most needs them, and reject him with a ferocity that leaves him numb with dismay. There is a loss of home, income, friends, colleagues, and security. There is a quiet devastating loss of status. "One day I was idolized in the parish," one priest says. "The next day I was washing dishes."

There is the horror of seeing the beloved Mother Church, which has been his life and breath, and his salvation, turn into a cruel stepmother that first spurns him like a cur and then denies his existence.

This is not to say that priests are the only ones who suffer so. Suffering is a part of life, a part of growing. The transition to adulthood frequently brings acute suffering, and much of what these priests endure is a delayed form of that suffering. And there are many other transitions in life that bring similar sorrow. Divorce is an obvious instance.

In fact leaving the ministry is rather like a divorce—where the parish is the spouse and the people are the offspring. There is, however, one way in which it can be harder than a divorce. If a doctor divorces, he remains a doctor. If he marries, he still keeps his role. A priest does not. But he loses something far more than a role—he loses his very identity. For a priest is so trained that his person and his ministry are one and the same. So he almost ceases to exist as a person and must try to build a totally new personality. It takes years and it takes tears.

"When you marry you want to rejoice, to scream it from the rooftops," says a priest's wife in Phoenix, Arizona. "Instead it is a march through hell." And many priests when they leave do not even have a partner to march beside them.

Of all the terrors of this path, probably the most awful is that until recently relatively few had trodden it. And fewer still had told of their experiences. There were no models, no examples for the priest to follow when he left. John Dubay, a married priest of Binghamton, New York, describes it: "It is a journey that has no historical precedent. . . . It is indeed dark night, since our journey has so few handholds or footholds to guide and direct our way. This sense of having no reference in reality by way of history, legacy, legend, experience, or knowledge, adds to the dark night."

In a sense, a Catholic priest who leaves takes with him neither a future nor a past. He has nothing—except his own strength of character, his personal qualities, and the grace of God. Yet these turn out to be enough.

When a priest leaves, the whole process is redolent of death. And a sense of bereavement swathes it like a shroud. "I thought I'd be burying you in your thirties," one father told his former priest son after he left. And when you look at a photo from those days, that son, now married and a father himself, does truly look as if he were terminally ill.

"Indeed it is a dying," says a married priest who had spent much of his ministry in terminal wards. "But it was my ministry that was terminally ill. There comes a stage where you grieve for the man that was, because you can never have that quality of life in the future. Kübler-Ross calls it *detachment*—pulling into oneself to weigh one's life."[1]

For the man who leaves, the acutest anguish usually comes before he decides, or before he acts on his decision. It is endured in silence and loneliness. And it can go on for years. The anguish is as Hamlet's: to be or not to be? What does God really want of me? What of scandal? What of hurt to parents and family and fellow priests and the bishop? Sometimes, quite often, there are thoughts of suicide. And sometimes, there is suicide.

So the idea of leaving the ministry is conceived in loneliness and born in isolation. The maturing can take years of silence.

Sometimes the priest does finally seek help from someone he trusts: maybe an older priest, a colleague he looks up to, or a priest during confession. Instead of help he may just get a stern lecture. Or worse, he may sense that the other man is having similar problems. What happens then is crucial. According to the sociologist Eugene Schallert, if no help is found, that is when he decides to leave, without perhaps fully realizing it. "Once that decision is made, he may develop a close relationship with a woman," Schallert says. And it could still take "an average of four to five years agonizing . . . before walking out of the door."[2]

Many priests experience a moment of truth. "Don't drag Jesus in the dirt," a Scottish Presbyterian minister in Glasgow told a priest friend who was having an affair. The priest went home and prayed, and that same evening asked the woman to marry him.

To try and decide whether to marry or remain a celibate priest, Frank Bonnike of Chicago went on a retreat, based on St. Ignatius's spiritual exercises. "The very first exercise had the words from the Scripture: 'This is everlasting life, to know God and His Son Jesus Christ.' Nothing about celibate priesthood. I couldn't get those words out of my mind. By the time of the fourth exercise, I went to the retreat master and said, 'I'm free.' "

Nature can bring a sense of proportion. The missionary Mick Caheny, returning to Europe from South America, stopped off at Easter Island. "I was brooding so much on Christ's words, 'He who hears you, hears me.' Are all these tiny Church rules covered by that mighty premise? Or is it being abused?

"But, looking at all those waves rolling in for three thousand miles, I felt the insignificance of so much. Here was I worried, thinking I was the center of the universe, and I was not. Here was I halfway between two continents. I felt I had a unique chance to size up everything. There were longings in me. I'd walk around and look at the stone statues. I went with the fishermen, and they'd cook the fish on stones on the shore. It was very paschal. I had a massive inundation of paschal and Gospel occurrences. It was like a great retreat: I relaxed in nature and stopped fighting against it."

After that Caheny returned to work in Ireland, where he had to wear black and where his monsignor in Athlone would not allow the priests to preach at their own masses. Caheny did not last long there.

A woman, if she enters a priest's existence amidst all this grieving and dying, is perceived and experienced as almost the quintessence of life. Often the transformation in the priest is dramatic. As a light bulb burns brighter in the last moments before it burns out, so a priest's ministry, in those last weeks or months before he leaves, is often noticed to be richer, more alive, more compassionate.

"Who is she?" Jim Peterman asked a fellow chaplain in Vietnam. The priest blustered that he didn't know what Jim was talking about. "Come on, Frank," Jim said. "There has to be a woman. You're being just too goddamn effective as a chaplain lately." Frank finally admitted that there was indeed a woman. Later he left to marry her.

At this point of course there comes a quite new kind of anguish—the struggle between this new life and celibacy. The relationship may be chaste, but it is driving inexorably toward marriage. A marriage that is unthinkable. This is the point where a woman can get hurt, if a priest becomes paralyzed by indecision. And the image of the callously scheming female, manipulating a simple cleric into matrimony, seems to be mostly myth. Too often she is the one manipulated.

It is also a point where a priest often takes what is called a "leave of absence." Technically, Church authorities allow him to opt out of the active ministry for a year or more, take a job, and think things over. Sometimes a priest returns at the end of the leave of absence, ready to resume ministry. More often he leaves for good.

I have found that the manner in which a priest leaves is important to later peace of mind. "I'm glad I didn't just run," an Irish resigned priest told me. "I'm glad I asked for a dispensation. And I'm glad I said good-bye to the lads and tried to explain it to them. That way we're still friends."

I met another man who did not leave like that. "The way I left was terribly wrong," he told me. "I just went over the wall, no note, nothing. Nobody knew where I was. It was bloody awful for me to have done it like that—I'm pained every time I think of the unnecessary distress to my family and to my fellow priests. I was just not man enough to face the option and say to the bishop, 'I want out.' If I could put the clock back, my mode of exit would be different. I believe in the infinite mercy of God—his arms extended on the Cross—but I find it harder, almost impossible, to forgive myself."

There is often a sense of euphoria when the priest actually does leave. One priest, now in counseling, thinks it's because most of the grieving has been done already: "There has been anticipatory grief. Like when watching a long-term illness of someone close to you (although in this case it's yourself): The muscle of the spirit has strengthened through constant exercising of grieving. By the time the rock drops, a person is better able to catch it and hold it. At least it doesn't crush."

But that first fine careless rapture doesn't last long. There are new pains to bear. The first of which, and it comes fast, is the loss of status. The second is loss of identity. And the third is poverty.

"I encountered poverty such as I had never known," a re-signed priest told me in Britain. "That first winter in London, I didn't have an overcoat. I was so poor I couldn't afford alcohol, although I had been drinking a lot before leaving. It was a helluva shock, going from inside to outside. I had been a Franciscan—I knew next to nothing about money: I didn't even know what a building society was for."

"After we married," Sicilian Antonio Corsello told me, "we had a year and a half of near destitution in Rome. Ina was pregnant. I wrote personally to the pope, telling of my hunger. The Vatican replied, sending me prayer and blessings. I wrote again that I couldn't live on that. Then they sent me fifteen thousand lire [about £10 sterling, or $14]. Imagine, fifteen thousand lire after twenty years of service."

In a book he has written about those days, Corsello says: "I looked for work in a thousand ways. Nothing. My clerical education had so 'incretined' me that even easy work was difficult for me. My way of presenting myself, my seminarist face, did not inspire con-fidence. . . . I came back home with empty hands, with great bit-terness. And with so much anger, that even now, after so many years, I still don't manage to soften it."[3] He also sought work and help in Church institutions and parishes. "I went in need," he writes, "but principally for a spiritual need: I needed personally to find out the level of charity that reigned in the centre of Catholicism. It was an interminable series of disillusionments, insensitivity and hardness of heart that bewildered me."[4]

The Corsellos had married in January. By the following Christ-mas they were living Bethlehem-like in the Torre Maura district of Rome. And close to starvation. "But news gets around," Corsello remembers. "Word got around the houses that here was a married priest with a pregnant wife, and hungry at Christmas. Well, the neighbours came in with everything—olives, cheese, sugar, the lot."

It was like the gifts of the Magi. "A neighbour saw us through the window, saw that we had nothing. She even brought us a Christ-mas tree. Do you know, we still use that tree every Christmas. And when Giulio was born, that woman became the godmother." Elvira Mastrosanti was the neighbor's name. I met her this last year, nearly two decades later, spending her vacation down in Sicily at the Corsello home. The Corsellos remember kindness too.

Corsello tells of one poorly dressed old woman who brought

him gifts that Christmas, "with such discretion and sensitivity that it moved me deeply." He later went to her little apartment to thank her and found her living in extreme poverty—"far worse than our own poverty," Corsello says.[5]

A few priests were kind, and Corsello insists that they be remembered. "Without their comfort," he says, "perhaps I would have definitively left the Catholic Church." Cardinal Pellegrino gave him help and comfort. There was a priest who telephoned a number of bishop friends begging a teaching post for Corsello, but without success. There was Don Balducci, who also tried to help. "I remember," Corsello writes, "the first time I told him my sad story, he was so moved that, trembling visibly and getting up from his chair, he came and embraced me tightly, so tightly that it seemed I could feel the beating of his great, noble heart. He said, 'Coraggio, Antonio. Non sei solo ["Courage, Antonio. You're not alone"].'

"Today I say, thank you, Don Balducci."[6]

Antonio Corsello is currently the national secretary of a powerful Italian trade union. The grim days are over. But for many resigned priests, especially in certain countries, that kind of poverty is their lot for the rest of their lives.

Poverty and unemployment is not, however, confined to those, for example, in the third world. I have met resigned priests in Britain who have enduring experiences of both. John Crawford-Leighton, a former warrant officer in the British military, and once in the priesthood, is married now and has not been able to find work in over ten years. The theologian Heinz-Jürgen Vogels has been unemployed for years in West Germany. I have encountered many other priests in Germany, Spain, Ireland, Italy, France, and throughout the United States who have had bleak and bitter experiences of unemployment.

One American married priest, now a prominent government administrator, told me of his years of unemployment, with a wife and two children to support. "I hit bottom one Christmas," he told me. "I got so mad at God that night—at least it shows I still believed—that I came home and threw away every religious object I had. How I've regretted that. How I wish to God I had my mission cross back. At least I have my rosary—I couldn't find it to throw it out.

"The day after Christmas I was sitting there talking of suicide. Luckily we had this wonderful old grandma: She came and slapped me across the face. She told me things about my own worth, and how much I had done in her life. She said I had been more a priest to her in the few months she was with us than any priest in her life.''

Job interviews hold particular terrors for a man who has served as a priest. In France, for example, when you go for an interview, you are a man without a history, the French priest-sociologist Julien Potel says. The years of priesthood have to remain hidden because French employers are scared stiff of ''marginal, confrontational types.''

The real miracle is that in spite of everything being loaded against them, the vast majority of resigned priests throughout the world do ultimately find themselves in worthwhile jobs, often in positions of high responsibility. In my contact list of resigned priests I find psychologists, doctors, social workers, personnel managers, journalists, editors, writers, filmmakers, radio producers, university professors in at least three continents, college lecturers, teachers, psychotherapists, government administrators, and civil servants, plus a mystery novelist, a police chief, a member of the West German parliament and an executive of Germany's Christian Democrat party, a provincial governor in Brazil, a millionaire inventor (who uses his millions for the poor), Greenland's negotiator with the European Community, a U.S. diplomat, a secret service agent, a vice president of General Mills and an Episcopalian bishop in Ecuador.

The preferred professions? Whichever deal with people rather than things. And especially professions that help. ''Nature breaks out through the eyes of the cat,'' as the Irish proverb says.

The very success of thousands of priests has itself led to changing attitudes, particularly in the United States. According to *The Wall Street Journal*, in a special news report on people and their jobs, ''ex-priests and nuns make excellent employees, many companies discover.'' The paper quotes a bank executive as saying, ''They're super performers, and are good at dealing with bureaucracy and office politics.''[7]

The completeness of this turnaround in attitude, at least in the United States, can be at least partly attributed to one man. Marty Hegarty is nothing short of an apostle of resigned priests and nuns: He has made it his life's work to help them get jobs after they leave. A Chicago priest until he left in 1969, Marty quickly built a name as an industrial psychologist, founding his own consulting firm.

With the independence it gave him, he set about helping his ex-clerical brothers and sisters in need of work. He founded an organization called WOERC, which has the single objective of finding jobs, and it has found them for many hundreds of resigned priests and nuns. Its principal tool is a regularly updated directory of the nation's resigned priests who already have jobs and are willing to provide job leads for others. The directory is backed up by a regular newsletter.

I went to see Marty Hegarty in his East Point apartment, eleven floors above Lake Michigan. I found a blunt, leathery man touching sixty, brimming with humor and quite devoid of sentimentality. "Woerc," he explained, is just the Old English spelling of "work" and pronounced the same. Simple. Why has he been so successful? By going just after jobs and staying out of all the campaigning for letting priests marry. Simple again. A narrow field of fire.

Above all, the media heed and report about Marty, and through the years he has hammered home the fact that priests make marvelous employees. So nowadays American priests face only the same level of prejudice as is met by military men or academics who look for jobs. As Marty says, "The expectation will be that the academic is too smart, the military man is too rigid, and the priest is too 'good.' "[8]

Priests who leave need counseling and advice, not just on work, but on all aspects of their transition. A Minneapolis group called Transition, founded by the married priest Gary Meitz, provides career assessment, job-seeking training, follow-up services, and women's support. Several resigned priests have told me their lives were practically saved by the Career Program Institute run by John Mulholland in Washington, D.C.

Britain has a group called New Bearings, founded to help priests and religious in transition. Even though it is a small organization, the advice and contacts that New Bearings provides have been a lifeline for many priests and nuns who leave.

In talking to many of these groups, I find they stress two basic pieces of advice for priests who are leaving. First, a priest should try to get a secular qualification, if at all possible, before leaving. Second, he should not just look for any old job to keep body and soul together. He should aim for a career, they say. And aim as high as he can: his potential will astonish him.

*   *   *

Sooner or later, then, with the passing of years, many of the priests who leave manage to get on their feet. They find careers, take wives, and father children. Much of the grief dwindles. But not all. There is one grief that can stay and stay for years, perhaps until a man dies. It is twofold: the grief and hurt of the family, and the grief of the priest when his family rejects him. The extraordinary ferocity of this rejection was mentioned by priests in every country I visited.

Sisters seem to take it hardest. "I have never seen my nephews and nieces in twelve years," Eoin, an Irish married priest, told me. Eoin's two sisters just don't want him around their families, and they certainly do not want his wife. "I was told, if you want to marry her, for God's sake go to Australia. They see my wife as the scarlet lady that led me out of the Church."

A man from the north of England speaks of what he calls the appearance of forgiveness: "Their attitude is, we forgive you, but do you realize you did something awful?" The effort is made, but it's only the glimmer of twilight, never glad confident morning again.

Joe Gerharz of Seattle told me shortly before his recent death how his family reacted to his leaving: "I was a priest in L.A. at the time, and my sister came down on a business trip. I told her I was going to grad school. She got up from the restaurant and walked out—she interpreted it as leaving the priesthood. She said, 'No matter what you do, don't ever tell Mother.'

"I did call my mom and told her I was going to graduate school. She said to me, 'He who puts his hand to the plow and looks back . . . If your father was alive he'd horsewhip you!'

"I'd never said this to Mom before, but I said it—'You goddamn sonovabitch,' I said to her, 'I'm going to do my thing and I never want to hear that from you again!' I slammed down the phone.

"She called right back. She said, 'Jody, I'm eighty years old and I'm dying, and I never want you to come home again, 'cause you'd be an embarrassment to your brother and sisters.' (Mom was Peg Burke, the daughter of Annie Mullarney from Ireland.)

"My brother called up a short time later: 'Mom tells me you're going to graduate school and that you might leave. I want to tell you I'm a businessman and I don't think you're tough enough to make it on the outside.'

"My younger sister called and said, 'The bishop who gets you your dispensation, and the pope who grants it, and the girl you're going to marry, and you yourself—you're all going to burn in hell.' ''

In 1983 Joe Gerharz's mother was dying in Billings, Montana. ''I walked into the hospital room and she said, 'Go and get your hair cut.' I spent three days listening to her at a deep level, during which she told me things I never knew. That she was the only one of eight children married in church, one of the few that was not an alky, the only one got an education. All this time I listened, listened, and we became good friends. One of the things I said to her in those days was, 'Y'know, Mom, it's because you taught me never to be satisfied, and always to search, that I now have courage to reexamine my life and make the changes I need to make.'

''The most beautiful thing [Joe is crying when he tells me this]—she called me over to the bed, and took my hand, and said, 'Jody, forgive me. I hope I haven't ruined your life.'

''She was a great little lady.''

Joe's younger sister died of cancer, without their being reconciled. Joe said, ''She was five months in hospital. I flew from Seattle every month to see her. She knew she was dying. The first time I came, the nun went in to see her first. 'Peggy, your brother's here. Don't you think it's time to reconcile?' 'I have time,' my sister said. She wouldn't talk.

''Every time I visited her, she would not talk. I'd sit there, holding her hand. One time I was sitting there looking at her. She turned. 'Quit staring at me,' she said. I was racking my brains— what can I do?

''I was back here in Seattle when she died. If I have any regret, it's for what happened to my sister. She made her choice. But I grieve that she lived with all that anger for so many years.''

And *I* grieve now for Joe. During my days in Seattle that gentle, sensitive man became my friend. And then he died suddenly, before I could get back to see him again.

It is the resigned priest's mother who usually suffers most. Mothers have been heard to say when a son leaves, ''I'd rather he had died.'' In fact the grief of such a mother is greater than bereavement, for to this grief there is added shame, public humiliation, where-did-I-go-wrong remorse, and fears for the eternal salvation of a son gone astray.

Yet over and over again it is the mother who finally reaches out when the long grieving is over. Sometimes the outcome can be beautiful and happy. A year after Joe and Cathy Grenier married, they took Joe's mother to live with them in Pennsylvania, and she was with them for five years until she died in 1986.

The birth of a child can often be the catalyst of reconciliation. There is a certain undeniability about children, even priest's children, and their very existence can bring the grandparents running.

A priest-colleague, still in the active ministry, can help a man's family toward acceptance and reconciliation, as the family will often take its cue from him. Would that more priests realized this. When one German missionary returned home with his bride, his parents were at Frankfurt airport to meet him. So too were several of his priest-colleagues, and their very presence was enough to reassure the parents and help the new relationships off to a healthy start. Indeed perhaps the greatest service fellow priests could render would be to provide a counseling service for parents and family of a priest who leaves. They frequently need it more than the priest himself.

But why in the first place is there such grieving and anger from the family? In fact it is understandable. One resigned priest who knew much rejection explained it to me: "They say those who mind don't matter, and those who matter don't mind. But that's not really true. There's a bereavement that has to go on in a family. The relationship was all bound up with your being a priest, and it has to be unraveled. It's a measure of their love for you that they mind so much."

A lot of the hurt has to do with status. In rural Ireland they used to say a family got respect from having "a pump in the yard, a bull in the field, and a son in the priesthood." To lose that son means acute humiliation, friends' looking away, neighbors sniggering and wagging their heads.

It can be traumatic if the "prodigal" comes home to visit. And yet that is the most effective healing of all. "The resigned priest must try to be present to the family as much as possible," one of them explained to me. "They deserve a chance to grieve with you and over you, every time they confront you, or are confronted by you in your new capacity. It's like with dying: The widow must have reminders of her husband, to push against, so to speak. Otherwise there's no draw on her grief.

"When I quit, one of my uncles took it very bad. The local

priest went to visit him and was rebuffed at the door—an unheard-of
occurrence. But my sister made it her business to talk about me
every time she could. 'I had a letter from Luke,' she would say to
the uncle. 'Wait till I tell you his news.' She was making me real to
him every time—giving him a chance to grieve.

"Then came a day when I knocked on his door. Uncle Jim
threw his arms around me and burst into tears. 'What was wrong
with me was pride,' he said."

CHAPTER 4

The Brethren and the Institution

When the Church prays for vocations, I think of Cain asking God for a new baby brother.

A U.S. priest

ONE morning in 1978, the priests and brothers of the Dominican Priory of Tallaght in Dublin, Ireland, stood around the altar to concelebrate mass. Later that day, six thousand miles away, one of their number would stand before another altar, awaiting his bride. In that Dublin monastery a young priest stepped forward to read the petitions: "Let us pray for David Rice, once a member of this community, who is getting married today in Portland, Oregon, that God may bless him and his bride and give them happiness. Lord hear us."

Around that altar forty voices answered, "Lord graciously hear us."

Some hours afterward, as my wedding began in St. Andrew's Church in Portland, I noticed a basket of flowers before the altar. The Interflora label read "From your Brethren."

If I should forget you, Dominicans, let my right hand be forgotten.

I was fortunate to have belonged to a group of enlightened men, members of a worldwide religious order ancient enough and great enough to act with magnanimity and even with love. That level of warmth and care for men who leave is not found in every religious order. Still less is it found in every local diocese.

It is understandable. Priests suffer almost like relatives when a colleague leaves and go through a similar process of bereavement.

Their grief and loneliness is one of the untold stories of the Church today. "It's like someone dying," one priest says. "Especially if you are good friends. It leaves a hole, a gap. And those holes in your life are never really filled. I am conscious of those holes as I grow older."

He says there is turmoil in the heart of a man who remains. "Should I go too?" he finds himself asking. "Or, what's wrong with us here, that he had to leave us?" You become acutely aware of the imperfections of your institution when someone leaves, he says.

At times like these it can sometimes require immense reserves of strength and personal faith to remain a priest, and the marvel is that so many do. One Jesuit identified for me three stages in a priest's reaction when a colleague leaves: "First *shock*—'Not So-and-so. He wouldn't leave. Impossible.' Then *denial* that it has happened—you just carry on as usual. Finally it becomes a *forbidden topic*—people who have left are, by consensus, not discussed. Or they are only spoken about in a restricted way—'I saw So-and-so down at the traffic lights today.' Reply: 'Oh?' And the conversation lapses.

"I believe," this priest continues, "that such communities need to go through a bereavement process. We need to sit down and talk it out, and work out our grief."

Bereavement of this magnitude can take years to heal, and it is understandable that some priests remain hurt and hostile. The hostility can range from pulpit to denunciations to cold indifference that lasts for years.

Paradoxically those who are understanding and warm to men who leave are usually the priests most fulfilled by their own priesthood and celibacy. Or those who have been through a crisis but have endured and grown. Often they seem to be men genuinely striving for spirituality.

An assistant pastor in a lonely parish in Ireland was "in the throes'' of deciding to leave and had no one to confide in. Finally he got up courage to tell his old parish priest. "Eventually I sat him down and I told him. The old boy thought for a while, and then he said, 'I've a bit of money put aside—you'll be welcome to it. And remember, you will always be welcome in my house, you *and whoever comes with you.*' Those were his exact words. That for me was a sign of resurrection. It was one of the best experiences of my life.''

I have come across individual priests who are true samaritans and are cherished by their married brothers. For example, down in Rio de Janeiro, the American oblate priest Ed Leising is a legend. In FASE, the educational and social assistance organization he founded in Brazil, he has given employment to 120 resigned priests since 1964. Some move on to other posts; some have remained as FASE administrators. "We are committing mortal sin," he told me bluntly, "by not using the talents of these men. Ninety-five percent of them have the deepest Christian belief, without a blink of doubt. We are educators, and I need people who can relate to others in terms of belief.''

There are individual bishops, too, who are true brothers to their married priests. When Augustin and Anne Marie Joseph went from Haiti to an international meeting of married priests in Rome, their trip was paid for by bishops in Haiti. The auxiliary Bishop Gerald Mahon of Westminster did the same for an English couple.

Archbishop Pat Flores of San Antonio has set out to be a peacemaker between the married and celibate priests of his still-wounded diocese. "I still want to be a friend to those who were my friends prior to their leaving," he told me in an interview. "I will not close the door on them, or my love or my heart to them, even if unfortunately I cannot offer them participation in liturgical services.''

There are some other bishops who try to do what they can, but like Nicodemus they can come out only at night. For they operate in a Kafkaesque climate of fear that has to be encountered to be believed. Over and over in my travels I have been told, please do not publish anything, or please do not identify me—look what they did to Hunthausen [the Archbishop of Seattle who was publicly deprived of his functions by the Vatican for, among other things, his supportive attitude to resigned priests].

On February 2, 1988, I had an appointment for an interview

with Cardinal Arns in São Paulo. I was presented to him in the hall
of the big old house that serves as diocesan offices. This is a journalist from Europe, the priests presenting me said. "Ah, good.
You're welcome," said the cardinal. A warm handshake for me.
He's a married priest, they said to Arns. *"Muito bem* ['That's
fine'],'' said Arns, and gave me a pat on the shoulder. He wants to
interview you on married priests, they told him. Arns stopped cold.
"Absolutely not," he snapped. "I do not give interviews on that
subject." And that was that.

Arns has in the past been a courageous and consistent cam-
paigner for a married ministry. It was explained to me that right then
he was under intense Vatican scrutiny. If he put a foot wrong he
could be whisked off to Rome and put in charge of some meaning-
less office, thus ending forever any further chance of accomplishing
anything for his beloved Brazil. He was not going to risk that for the
likes of you, the Brazilians explained gently.

In the matter of priests leaving and priests marrying, this fear
pervades the Roman Catholic Church from top to bottom, as if it
were the Kremlin. At the top it is fear of loss of office, or loss of
promotion; in places like Africa it is fear of losing Rome's financial
support; at the bottom of the heap it is a fear of dismissal, home-
lessness, and destitution. And sometimes of suicide. And those
fears have grounds.

When I began research for this book, I thought I would encounter a series of heartwarming stories of kindness from merciful
Church authorities, reaching out to brothers who were hurting, as
the Dominicans in so many ways reached out to me. What I found
instead was that the deeper into the institutional Church I penetrated
and the higher up the pyramid of Church authority I went, the more
indifference and sometimes cruelty I encountered.

Institutions can do strange things when they sense a need to
protect themselves, and the Catholic Church, composed of human
beings, is no exception. But in the light of its mission of spreading
God's love, some of the things it does are very strange indeed.

There is a word that lies deep in the memory of the Irish
people, a word that still sends a shiver down their spines. That word
is "eviction." It evokes images of a ragged family huddled in the
cold; of bailiffs with battering rams sent by a cruel landlord to
demolish the thatched cottage; of helmeted police holding back the

sullen crowd; of the arrogant sheriff astride his horse with the eviction order in his hand.

This century-old scene came to life once more on December
11, 1981, in the Dublin suburb of Templeogue. There were some
differences this time: The sullen crowd wore modern jeans and
carried umbrellas, and the police wore civilized caps instead of
helmets. It wasn't a thatched cottage, but a suburban duplex, on the
front door of which television cameras focused. The sheriff as he
climbed out of his Mercedes wore a natty business suit and tie.

Also there were two other differences: The man waiting inside
to be evicted wore a black suit and a Roman collar; and the landlord
who had called in the sheriff to evict him was His Grace, Most Rev-
erend Dermot Ryan, archbishop of Dublin and primate of Ireland.

The priest was Mayo-born Fr. Michael Keane, and he was
being evicted from his rectory because the archbishop had suspended him and ordered him out. A Dublin diocesan spokesman
told me that the archbishop "had agonized an awful lot before
taking the decision to evict" and had waited four years before doing
so. However, what shocked the people of Ireland was that an archbishop would evict a priest under any circumstances, that Mother
Church would do that to one of her children, one of her priests, for
any reason whatsoever. As another active priest Brendan Hoban
wrote in the *Western People* newspaper: "What about all the theory
we hear about community and love and brotherhood? What about all
the sermons we hear on forgiveness and Christian reconciliation?
What about the scripture quotation about turning the other cheek,
going the extra mile, giving your cloak as well as your coat? Or is
the preaching (people ask) not for the preachers, too? Is keeping the
clergy in line such a priority in our church that our leaders prefer to
place their faith in a civil court before the Gospel of love that Christ
preached?"[1]

The answer would sometimes seem to be *yes*. In 1969 in Cleve-
land, Ohio, two priests were celebrating an unauthorized protest
mass at which they were going to read a statement on racism,
poverty, and war. The diocesan office, an official of which was
chaplain to the police, had word that something was going to take
place. One of the two priests told me what ensued. "By the time we
got to the offertory, all the people but one couple had been removed,
and there were about forty cops around the altar rails. It came to
communion time. We had to give communion to the couple still

there. We had to go through the ranks: It came to scuffles and the Host went flying. I was dragged out and carried away in the paddy wagon, still in my vestments.''

That priest now works as a layman in Seattle; the other was later reinstated in the diocese.

In Italy they speak of the "White Homicides" of the Church. It was the priest-journalist Gianni Gennari who coined the phrase to describe Italian Church cruelty and indifference to priests and nuns who leave.

In an article in the daily *Paese Sera,* Gennari printed a letter from a nun who had left her cloister after twenty-three years. She had taught during those years in the convent's school and had no pension. Her letter reads: "Fourteen years wandering the streets of the city, seeking home and work; nine changes of residence; four years completely unemployed and in despair. A few days ago I fell at the feet of the superiors, begging for work in the institute's school, since I had no other possibility. I was told an ex-sister could no longer teach. . . . I'm hungry. . . . At another institute I asked for help, and was rejected. Am I to die in despair?"[2]

In the same article Gennari tells of another nun who also left and who finished as a prostitute on the streets of Florence. Gennari has her name, and the name of the priest who found and rescued her.

He writes of people leaving religious life after ten years, "with 500,000 lire and *arrivederci.*" That figure is about £250, or $300. In the last twenty years, Gennari says, thousands of nuns and priests have found themselves thus, "without guarantees and without social dignity, forgotten by all, regarded with suspicion by their brethren and by those who had shared their lives for years, treated as half-men and half-women, worms and no men, as the scripture had said.

"Only God remains to them, and the friendship of those who reject that terrible law that values the institute more than the person, good name more than gospel, and appearance more than substance. They are abandoned to themselves, annuled both in memory and in friendship, so that it can be said with ferocity, 'Look what a fate you have, if you are not faithful.' ''[3]

It is the equivalent of homicide, Gennari says. It goes back a long way. Giustino Zampini, now a very old man living in Genoa, was forced to live as a vagrant, sleeping in doorways and under bridges, after leaving the ministry over fifty years ago.

It was not always a matter of mere Church indifference to the fate of the "lapsed" one: Sometimes these men were vigorously pursued and deliberately deprived of work by Church authorities, even when they were in state employment. The 1929 Concordat between the Vatican and the Italian government has the following article:

> Art 5. No ecclesiastic may take up, or remain in, employment or office of the Italian State or public bodies depending on the State, without the *nihil obstat* ["permission"] of the Ordinary [bishop] of his diocese. The revocation of the *nihil obstat* deprives the ecclesiastic of the capacity of continuing to exercise such employment or office. In no case may apostate priests, or those subject to censures, take up or continue in a post as teacher, or in an office or employment in which they will come into a direct contact with the public.[4]

From the moment the concordat was signed, a bishop could actually call on the Italian state to dismiss a resigned priest from state employment. Could and did.

A tragic instance is that of Ernesto Buonaiuti, who has been called "the most excommunicated man in the history of the Church." Accused of modernism early in the century, he was hounded from job to job.[5]

In 1906, at the age of twenty-five, he was dismissed from his post as lecturer in Church history in the pontifical major seminary in Rome, after the review, *Civiltà Cattolica,* had attacked his teaching. Thence his life was one long ordeal of being suspected, interrogated, threatened, condemned. He continued always to pray and to wear priest's clothes, in spite of several excommunications that followed.

In 1915 Buonaiuti secured a post outside the reach of the Vatican—that of professor of the history of religion at the University of Rome. However, one year later, when it seemed he might die after a medical operation, Cardinal Gasparri visited him in his hospital bed and offered him Holy Communion, *on condition* that he gave up his university post. Buonaiuti refused, and was refused communion.

In 1926 he was declared *excommunicatus vitandus*. This was both an excommunication and an official Church sentence of boycott. Catholics were required to shun a person so excommunicated, to avoid such a person absolutely, even in professional or social contacts. This meant that no Catholic could attend Buonaiuti's university lectures, and it forced the university to move him out of teaching altogether. He was given editing work by the university authorities.

Then in 1929 the concordat was signed between Mussolini's Italy and the Vatican. Incredibly it contained the article that seemed made to measure against Buonaiuti, Article 5. Article 29 was also made to measure for a man who persisted in wearing clerical clothes and collar:

> Art. 29 (i). The use of the ecclesiastical and religious habit by laymen or by ecclesiastics or religious who have been definitely forbidden to wear it by the competent ecclesiastical authorities (who should officially communicate the fact to the Italian Government), is forbidden, and shall be punished with the same sanctions and penalties with which is forbidden and punished the improper use of military uniform.[6]

Not long afterward, the secretary of the Fascist party had an audience with Pope Pius XI. A week later Buonaiuti was called in by a government minister, who referred expressly to the secretary's meeting with the pope and ordered Buonaiuti to stop wearing clerical clothes. "Professor," he said, "you are aware of Article Twenty-nine of the concordat. It provides for the arrest of anyone wearing ecclesiastical garb while under excommunication. If you do not comply, the government will be obliged to proceed against you."

The following year Buonaiuti was dismissed from his university post, ostensibly for refusing an oath of loyalty to fascism.

Ernesto Buonaiuti died on Holy Saturday 1946 and was buried without any exterior sign of religion. He had written, years before, that the thought of leaving the Church filled him with "an obscure terror," as it would have abandoned him to "the dizziness of a lay world, empty of any spiritual consistency and of any Christian idealism."

Even after all his excommunications and suspensions, he continued to say the rosary daily with his mother until she died and, for her sake, to leave the house every morning as though he were going to celebrate mass.

The concordat has recently been replaced, but old ways die hard. Last year Don la Bella, a parish priest in Schiacca, Sicily, took me to a local café that is run by a married priest. "After the priest left the diocese to marry," la Bella said, "he asked the bishop if he could teach Christian doctrine in the local school. The bishop consulted his priests. I was all for it. The others, no. So he didn't get the job. His wife's people had this café. So now he runs that."

Rosario Mocciaro, a married priest in Rome, told me: "There are still many cases in Italy where married priests cannot get work teaching religion. And this, even under the new concordat we have. The problem is, for many of these priests, it's the only way they know how to live. And especially if they don't manage to get a dispensation after they leave, they are immediately fired from teaching religion. But dispensations are nearly impossible to get."

Mocciaro told me that teachers of religion, even in state schools, are still regularly nominated by the local bishop, so even there the same old problems arise for resigned and married priests.

In Holland, a high-ranking cleric asked the University of Utrecht to fire seven professors who were married priests. Three have now resigned of their own accord.[7]

In Fortaleza, Brazil, the papal nuncio ordered Cardinal Lorscheider to fire three professors at his seminary for the same reason. (One of them told me what happened there: "Cardinal Lorscheider replied that if the nuncio would provide him with three other teachers, he would obey the nuncio's wishes. Otherwise, he would keep them and take all the responsibility for it!" They're still there.)[8]

A married priest, Francis McNutt, still a distinguished figure in the Christian healing ministry, was struck from the list of speakers at a West Coast conference after a bishop objected. At a healing and prayer seminar, another bishop called officials and threatened to cut off funding if McNutt remained on the program.[9]

A Sri Lankan priest writes: "I know cases where, when prospective employers refer to the superiors about an ex-priest, he has really been condemned. I am glad to say that now some bishops and superiors take a more sympathetic view."[10]

John Dubay, a married priest and family psychotherapist in

Binghamton, New York, has worked for years with priests leaving the ministry. He speaks of his concern "for those men who were honest or attempted honesty in their resignation from the active priesthood and were treated in a monstrous, unchristian, and inhuman manner by fellow clerics. The range of stories approaches the absurd," Dubay writes, "when we learn of the devices of evil that were brought against them by men of God. Men have spoken of phone calls from the diocesan office at 2 A.M. to their family residence. Others have spoken of pressure on prospective employers, possibly with the hope that if unsuccessful at work, they would return to the active priesthood.

"Transcripts have been withheld by some bishops' offices, presenting difficulties in pursuing education, getting employed or licensed for employment. When asked of this by one married priest who needed work to support a wife and four children, the bishop's office responded that it was not their problem and should have been considered at resignation time."

John Dubay is describing the treatment that resigned priests encountered in the sixties and seventies, the decades following the Second Vatican Council. Bad though it may have been, it is nothing compared to the way such priests were treated before the council. Fr. Paul Winninger, writing in 1963 for the bishops of the council, describes it:

> The situation of these unfortunates is horrible. . . . We have succeeded in creating around them a . . . myth of the infected. . . . They themselves seem to be dumb with stupor, and bury themselves in silence, renouncing to defend themselves.
>
> Will no Father of the Council have the heart to become their advocate? Their misdeed does not deserve such a punishment, and this sentence is not worthy of the Church. Such a sanction is not that given by a mother. It is interpreted today as a brutal reaction, similar to that of parents who reject their child, an unwed mother for instance, who has "dishonoured" them.
>
> Authoritative voices assure us that the Church carries sorrowfully the burden of these "fallen priests." That is not true, since she excommunicates them. . . .
>
> In countries (Italy, Spain) where civil law recognizes

only the religious marriage of baptized persons, the injustice reaches a rare extreme: *these priests cannot get married even under civil law.* Deprived of religious rights and excluded from the Church, deprived simultaneously of essential civil rights and banned from society, with wife and children, they answer perfectly the definition of the infamous untouchable: the pariah. Indeed, the only example of a pariah in Western civilization is a Catholic product, and they are priests.

Is there an international tribunal to avenge the rights of man? If so, these priests can well bring their case to such a court.[11]

Several priests have told me of the one thing that keeps men in line—the fear of losing their pension and insurance. One of them put it thus: "Once you retire, you have your pension. Marry, and they cut it off. If I serve faithfully for seventy-five years, I'll be ninety-five or hundred years old. I marry—and they'll cut me off. They'll say, 'Old man, how dare you quit on us!' "

One of the saddest of all ecclesiastical cruelties I have encountered is what I call the "Cow Syndrome." It hurts women as well as men. When I was a very young priest trying to cope with celibacy, an older priest passed on to me a well-worn piece of wisdom: "Always remember, young Rice, if you want a glass of milk, you don't have to buy the bloody cow."

It is an attitude that can poison the personal life of a priest, but when it emerges as part of official policy—or rather, unofficial policy—it poisons the Church itself. In its policy form it amounts to Church demands that a priest abandon his wife and children. I quote a letter[12] from a certain U.S. bishop to one of his priests who had "strayed":

Dear——,
It was with great sadness that I learned of your decision to leave the priesthood and attempt marriage. As your bishop I am required to inform you that you have violated the canons of the Church which regulate your clerical life. You are in violation of canon 2388, 188, 132 #1, 1072

and therefore having attempted marriage you are now
excommunicated "latae sententiae."
If after receiving this letter and having given its contents
thought and prayer you wish to return to the clerical state,
you must leave your wife and your children if any *[italics*
mine] and obtain a civil divorce and do penance. After a
period of time we will apply to the Holy See for re-
instatement to the clerical state on your behalf.
With every best wish.

_____

Bishop of _____

Dr. Heinz-Jürgen Vogels, a married priest of Bonn, Germany, was sent a letter in 1983 by the vicar-general of the Archbishop of Cologne. It informed him that the Vatican's Cardinal Ratzinger had stated he could never return to priestly duties. However, even if he ever wants merely to have his excommunication lifted and return to the Church as a layman, "you must stop living with your wife, as you are only civilly married, without Church permission and against the norms of Church law. If you can come to an unequivocal decision, both to renounce any claim to priestly rights and powers, and also to seek a release from your marriage obligations, then the Congregation of the Faith will recommend to the Holy Father the granting of a dispensation [the reduction to the lay state]."[13]

This means that Vogels would lose both his priesthood and his wife as the price of reconciliation with the Church. And tragically that is precisely what happened. Vogels pined so much for peace with his Church that he did what the Vatican demanded and divorced Renata. He still lives with her, but in a "state of divorce."

The Vatican had no reason to demand that Vogels leave his wife: Her previous marriage had already been annulled by a Catholic Church court, so it had been no impediment to her marrying Vogels.

I stayed with Heinz and Renata for a few days last year and found two intensely prayerful Christians. But both also suffer intensely from a Church cruelty that is almost Byzantine. And Vogels has never got back his Church editing job—he had been part of a team preparing the definitive edition of the complete works of Albert the Great. As late as February 1989, Cardinal Ratzinger met Vogels in Rome and promised to speak in favor of his reemployment in that job. However in April 1989 Vogels got a letter from

Cologne's new Cardinal Meisner, saying there was no possibility of his reinstatement, and asking him nevertheless to stick to his original promise of celibacy. So this gifted German theologian remains unemployed.

A constant source of suffering for priests who leave is the curious process that used to go under the term "laicization" and is now more frequently called "dispensation." Put very briefly, it is official Vatican permission to leave the formal ministry. However, Church officials have often made it a lot more than that: It has been termed "a reduction to the lay state." But how can a man be thus reduced if he had been made "a priest forever"? Besides, the document of laicization states that in danger of death this "layman" must give the sacrament of reconciliation. Which is something only a priest can do.

However, that is far from being the only complication of this strange matter. The journalist Gianni Gennari in 1984 published in an Italian newspaper "A Christmas Letter to the Pope," accusing him of a triple unfairness to priests who marry. First, Gennari told the pope, you won't allow priests to marry without getting a dispensation to leave the ministry. Then you refuse that dispensation. Third, after refusing the dispensation, you insult them by saying they are in an unlawful condition.[14]

"*Vergogna*," roars the Sicilian married priest Antonio Corsello as he tramps with me across the black volcanic slopes of Etna, high above Linguaglossa. "I say *vergogna,* shame! Shame on the pope for what he has done to us married priests. The pope has a Christian duty to take people out of their sin. But by refusing dispensations to priests who have left and married, he is forcing these men into a state of sin. And then he keeps them there. Christ came to save, and this man is forcing them into sin. Where is the Christianity?"

The president of the Brazilian bishops, Dom Luciano Mendes, told a meeting of Brazil's married priests in May 1987 that it depends on who in Rome handles the application for dispensation. If it hits one particular desk, it moves faster; another desk, and it just crawls. So it's not surprising, he observed, that the results are often against all expectation.[15]

But is it in fact true that the present pope has practically cut off any hope of getting a dispensation? Has there in fact been a cutback?

Jim Cantwell, the press officer for the Dublin archdiocese, says there has. "Under Pope Paul the Sixth, dispensations were given fairly routinely," he says. "But an analysis of the situation would reveal that in some cases a person had entered a marriage that he was unable to sustain, or after a while has wished to return to the ministry. So there have been cutbacks."[16]

I hardly met a priest, resigned or active, around the world, who would accept this explanation. "It just drives priests into the registry office [courthouse] to get married," one man says. "It doesn't keep them in the priesthood. And if it does, then it's even worse. If a man remains a priest only because he can't get a dispensation, then he'd be like a trapped animal. What kind of use would he be as a priest then?"

Yet the pope, asked recently by a group of U.S. bishops to speed up the process of dispensation, replied, "I'm in no hurry. They left us: we didn't leave them."[17]

The pope is indeed in no hurry. One married priest penetrated the Vatican as far as to meet an official in Cardinal Ratzinger's office. That blond young German cleric told him there is no likelihood of dispensation "until you are on your deathbed."[18]

The whole application process for laicization is both demeaning and offensive. For the application to have the slightest chance, you have to admit to being either bad or mad, or that you should never have been a priest in the first place. In other words, that you are devoid of sexual control; or that you are a psychiatric case; or that you were pressured to become a priest. The whole thing is copied crudely from the marriage annulment process.

A missionary in Lima, Peru told me how he had to give evidence before a tribunal on behalf of a colleague who wanted to get dispensation. The findings of the tribunal would be forwarded to Rome. "He needed the dispensation because the wife wanted a church wedding. Well, I had to witness that he should never have been a priest. They warned me, there's no point in going in there and saying he was a great guy. You'll help him by saying negative things. It was the only way. It was as if we were imitating the Russian show trials."

An Italian married priest says that Church authorities in Rome told him the dispensation would be speeded up if he went to a psychiatrist and got a certificate to say he was mentally ill. A monsignor advised him how to comport himself for the psychiatrist: "Be sure to talk angrily, and to switch from smiling to weeping." The monsignor wrote out on a Church letterhead the addresses of two psychiatrists.

What that man says is amply borne out by a questionnaire that has been administered to priests wanting to leave a certain religious order in the United States. The following are some of the forty-three questions it contains:

9. How old were you when you entered the order?

10. Did you freely enter the Order or were you influenced by others to enter the Order? If you were influenced by others, who were they?

11. What was your parents' attitude toward your entrance to religious life and the priesthood?

13. Prior to your solemn profession, did you know the obligations flowing from the solemn profession and from the law of celibacy?

14. Prior to your entrance into the Order and during your years of religious and priestly formation, did you experience difficulties regarding chastity?

16. Are these same difficulties leading you to petition for laicization and a dispensation from your vows and the law of celibacy?

18. Were you doubtful about your vocation during your years of formation? Do you feel that you took adequate means to overcome these doubts at that time? Around what did these vocational doubts center?

23. After you were ordained, were you or are you troubled by moral problems relating to the vow and virtue of chastity and the law of celibacy?

24. Do you or did you experience any problems with drinking? Are you an alcoholic?

40. Have you suffered from any emotional disturbances or mental illness? If so, please specify.

41. Have you contacted any doctor or psychologist or professional counselor about your decision to leave the priesthood and religious life? If so, do you have a document or statement from him regarding this decision or will you sign a document releasing him from the obligation of professional secrecy and authorizing him to make such a statement in support of your petition?[19]

These questions clearly invite the petitioner to declare that he did not become a priest freely but was influenced by others; that he could not keep sexual control of himself both before and after his ordination; that he had emotional, mental, or alcoholic problems. It is also clear that a psychiatrist's declaration to that effect would help the matter of dispensation. In other words, if you want to leave, you'd better be bad or mad, or never have been freely ordained. Because only such people could possibly want to leave. . . .

In all of this the Church is no different from any other organization. Ralph Dahrendorf and other sociologists point out that any group will defend itself against rebellious or threatening members by declaring them either ill or amoral.[20] The point is, however, that the Church came to teach a new and different way, that of Gospel love.

The dispensation, if it ever comes, can be as humiliating as the application process. It claims to be a "reduction to the lay state." Even if one were to accept that it is really a return to the lay state, and that such a return is a "reduction," in fact the person "laicized" is reduced below the level of a lay person.

He is expressly excluded from many functions open to lay people. He cannot be a eucharistic minister; he cannot read the lesson in church. An official instruction from the Vatican's Congregation for the Faith (formerly the Holy Inquisition) expressly forbids "laicized" priests from "taking any liturgical part in celebrations with a congregation where his situation is known; he may never preach the homily." It also forbids him to occupy any administrative office in seminaries or similar institutes, or to teach there. "Likewise he shall not occupy the office of director of Catholic schools, or religion teacher in any schools, Catholic or otherwise."[21]

According to the same document a priest who is laicized "should not stay in a place where he was known as a priest." If the wretch chooses to marry, the bishop "should take care that pomp and display are avoided and that it take place before an approved priest and without witnesses, or if need be, two witnesses. The marriage should be recorded in the secret archive of the diocesan curia."

This secrecy would seem to contradict the very nature of marriage, which is essentially a public act.

The Church's 1983 revised book of laws (called the New Code

of Canon Law) makes things even more complicated. While now in cases of emergency it allows lay people to perform various ministries according to need, laicized priests are to be deprived "of all offices, functions, and any delegated power" (Can. 292).[22]

However it is far from clear where the new code really stands. Canon lawyers see it as riddled with loopholes, and some of them have been studying it at Catholic University of America to see if it can be used to the advantage of laicized priests.

I asked Dom Angelico Sandalo Bernardino, the auxiliary bishop of São Paulo, Brazil, what he thought of the whole dispensation circus. While infinitely cautious, he seemed not to take it all too seriously. "This whole problem of laicization is just a legal measure," he told me. "The priest continues as a priest: There's no doubt of this. At the present moment [Rome is] acting in this way. In Paul the Sixth's time, things were one way; now they are another. In the near future it could be different again. There used to be no way out at all. Then came a way out. This is a big advance, and if we practice holiness, authentic Christian life, and fraternal dialogue, there will be new steps forward. I don't know when, but the Holy Spirit always illuminates."

So why right now does anyone bother even asking for laicization? One reason is that you can't have a church marriage without it. Another reason is that a priest is excluded from many jobs if he is not laicized. His wife can be excluded too. In a California diocese, for example, a priest's wife applied for the principalship of a Catholic school and got the post. But, her husband tells me, the diocese found out that her husband was a married priest without dispensation. "The offer was pulled immediately," he says.

A book, published by Gooi & Sticht in Holland in 1986 entitled *Pastor*, lists eighteen points that are required by Church authorities in people seeking to work in any church-related field. They were put together from accumulated pastoral experience of the previous ten years in Holland and have been neither denied nor conceded by Dutch Church authorities.[23]

Some of the eighteen points are explicit against married priests. Those without a dispensation are totally excluded from consideration. And since the Dutch Synod in 1980, even priests *with* dispensation can no longer be nominated *in any role whatsoever*.

Yet by giving a dispensation, the Church is releasing a man from his promise and declaring that promise nonexistent. The married priest Antony Padovano asks, "Why then are we punished, and God's people with us? Would any of us release a child from a promise and then punish the child?"

Apart from the question of employment, laicization is still a matter of conscience for many priests who leave. I met a man who left many years ago and has now been waiting seven years to marry the woman he loves. "But the law is important to me," he says. "I want laicization before I marry Diane. If I went ahead without it, I feel I'd be cutting my lifeline to God." So far there is not the sniff of a dispensation.

For some men who do marry, the waiting for a dispensation that never comes is like Kafka's man waiting all his life, until he dies, for permission to enter the castle. It can bring a lifetime of anguish and it has led, in cases that I personally know, to marriages breaking up.

It is not surprising then that more and more priests are simply not bothering to ask for laicization. It's just no longer important to them.

Even the people are going their own way. In Recife, Brazil, the Holy Ghost missionary Brian Eyre was preparing to marry a local girl. He says: "The day before the wedding, the people organized a concelebrated mass in my church and invited all the neighboring priests. Four came. So did Marta's parents and brothers and sisters. The church was absolutely full of people, with Marta and me sitting down among them. At one point, the people called us to the front of the church, and everybody put their hands over us and they said, 'Even if the official Church won't give you a blessing, we, the people of God, give you our blessing.' The next day we had the civil wedding at her parents' house."

In its human dimension, the Church is a group like any other. When there is internal conflict, a group will defend itself by neutralizing or expelling the troublesome ones. A group's harshness is however usually softened by structures like courts and juries to ensure fair play. But the Church has not yet developed such structures, so there is nothing to save the individual from the full fury of its defense mechanisms.

But there is more to the Church than the merely human dimension. It happens to be a community that derives from Jesus Christ, He who taught that the Sabbath was made for people, not people for the Sabbath. The Church's real crisis lies in ignoring that very instruction. The great Trappist monk Thomas Merton speaks of "the crisis of authority brought on by the fact that the Church, as institution and organization, has in fact usurped the place of the Church as a community of persons united in love and in Christ. Love is equated with obedience and conformity within the framework of an impersonal corporation. The Church is preached as a communion, but is run in fact as a collectivity, and even as a totalitarian collectivity."

We speak of *ecclesia semper reformanda* ("the Church forever in need of reform"). Jesus taught that "by this shall all people know that you are my disciples, that you love one another." That love is already richly alive among Church members as individuals, at whatever level they are found, and there are many moving instances of it. But that same love now needs to percolate upward through the structures, transforming them to the words of Christ: "Do not lord it over them as the Gentiles do." So far it has signally failed to do so.

One married priest wonders if that could explain the puzzle of "a Church of beautiful persons, but who have a public or ecclesiastical *persona*—a sort of group personality, if you like—that is far from beautiful. It's almost like ecclesiastical schizophrenia," he says. The old Latin saying is apt in this context—*canonici boni viri; capitulum autem mala bestia* ("the priests of the cathedral chapter are decent fellows; but the chapter itself is a wicked beast").

"There's a scene in Brecht's *Galileo Galilei,*" a married priest recalls, "where Galileo is talking to the pope. The pope is enthused by Galileo's theories. . . . A rapport begins to develop between the two men. Then the pope dresses to leave. As each vestment goes on him, the rapport diminishes. The whole texture of the pope's language alters. . . . He begins to cite Scripture, to cite Ecclesiastes.

"The man begins to recede, and the officeholder is standing there, condemning. The rapport ends in canon law and censure, and finally the pontiff is standing there, denouncing, accusing, condemning."

Eppur, se muove.

CHAPTER 5

A Priest Forever?

Kai sat still and cold. Then little Gerda cried, and her tears fell on Kai's breast. The warmth penetrated to his heart and melted both the ice and the glass-splinter in it. Kai burst into tears and wept so much that the grains of glass in his eyes were washed away. . . . Gerda kissed him on his cheeks and the colour came back to them. She kissed his eyes and they became like hers. He became well and strong.
　　　　　Hans Christian Andersen, "The Snow Queen"

ONCE upon a time an Irish priest was traveling by train across the United States. Down by some shunting yards, somewhere in the Midwest, he came face to face with an old hobo who was climbing out of a boxcar. Their eyes met and held. *"Tu es sacerdos in aeternum,"* the Irishman said. A statement, not a question—"Thou art a priest forever." And the old man nodded.

Men who were once ordained really do seem to stay priests forever. Abstracting from the theology of it, one could say there are subtle, and not so subtle, marks about such men, which they never seem to lose. And their wives are the first to point out that priesthood leaves its mark. "Financially they are hopeless," one wife says. "They haven't a bull's notion about money. Sometimes it would drive you out of your mind."

"Priests aren't very practical husbands," another wife adds. "All their training is intellectual, and idealism can be rather cloying. It could frustrate some wives, because they never get that material wealth that they would have had if their husbands had more drive. There's a lack of ruthlessness in most of them—I mean, idealism doesn't wash in business, where promotion is important."

The men themselves mostly admit not to be wildly ambitious. "I just can't shake off St. Augustine's words, which I lived by for so long—'It's better to need little than to have much,' " one of them explains.

Does that mean he'd let his wife and kids be poor?

"Certainly not. Poverty has its own anxieties. It's just a question of moderation. For me, success isn't measured in promotion or praise. Success, rather, is being really useful," he says. "It's getting results, or seeing someone's face light up when you're able to help them."

But it would be a mistake to think that these men don't care about success: For them it is probably the most important thing of all. "When you were a priest, society had you on a pedestal," one recalls. "So you feel stripped of a sacred overlay, and you need some sort of success to restore your sense of worth." It's just that these men seem to have slightly unconventional notions of success. And they seem happiest in service-oriented jobs. Those in business often give leisure time to working for others like the aged or the poor, or they do some counseling.

The priests who leave to marry are frequently men of outstanding potential—potential winners rather than losers. But they do have a lot of developing to do.

To begin with, they come from a particularly gifted group of men. A couple of decades ago you could not even have made it through seminary without being intellectually well endowed. Ray Henke recalls IQs of 130 as not unusual in the San Antonio seminary. "I taught there and simultaneously at a Catholic university," he recalls. "It was unbelievable the difference. There wasn't a single course at the university with the same abstractive level as we had at the seminary."

The men entering in those days were also mostly what the Americans call "jocks"—popular, athletic, most-likely-to-succeed types. Several priests, including a vocation director, tell me this type flooded the seminaries from the end of World War II until the early seventies. Some think these youngsters were attracted by the heroism of the wartime chaplains, but they certainly shattered the Victorian stereotype of the priest as a genteel wimp in skirts.

A clerical and seminary environment, however, could hold back the emotional development of even such a gifted group of men. In the early 1970s, the psychologists Eugene Kennedy and Victor Heckler were asked by the U.S. bishops to do a socio-psychological profile of the American priest.[1] They found only 6 percent of priests fully mature and developed, while 29 percent were in the process of growing and developing, 57 percent were underdeveloped, and 8 percent were maldeveloped. These figures were thought to derive from certain unfortunate aspects of seminary training. As Kennedy and Heckler explain it in their book published by the U.S. bishops' Catholic Conference: "Their difficulties are precisely those you would expect if you took a group of young men, sent them to special schools, virtually eliminated their contact with women, and then put them to work in circumstances that continued to reinforce all-male living in a socially restricted public religious role."[2]

In a talk he gave in Los Angeles, Kennedy further pointed out that at least 80 percent of those who leave come from that *developing* category. These are people who "have had their personal growth suspended or delayed, and now, through circumstances or personal decisions, find themselves challenged anew by the problems of growth."[3] In these priests one can see vitality, a sense of purpose, and a determination to move forward in personal development:

> Some event, or series of events . . . reactivate the dormant development processes. Common experiences that lead to development are a new job or work assignment, death of one's parents, especially the mother, new educational experiences, the effect of Vatican II, a serious failure, a profound religious or personal experience, particularly with a woman. This realm of personal experience is probably the most potent and frequent force in reinitiating growth in the life history of the individual develop-

ing priest. Such a confrontation leads the person more deeply into himself than he has ever been before. He begins to put aside the very controlling defences with which he has restricted his life experiences, and he moves into human realms that he can truly say he never knew existed before this kind of experience occurred.[4]

Some of these men remain in the ministry and mature into outstanding priests. Others find that their growing and maturing continues in the context of marriage, family, and the workplace. These are the men who leave. Their maturing can take years and it can be very painful. There is anger and guilt to be faced and dealt with. But more than anything there is the building up of a new person, a new identity.

When he was of a dangerously early age, the seminary set out to bond together the young man and his priestly or clerical role so tightly that they were almost one flesh. It succeeded so well that a man has almost to flay himself alive to discard that clerical skin. "I was trying to integrate my mind and emotions," Mick Caheny of São Paulo tells me. "I was trying to deinstitutionalize myself. It was like peeling an onion: The more you took off, the more you cried. In the end I felt like Adam coming from the hand of God," lying there raw and new, waiting to be touched into life.

Some priests actually changed their names after leaving in an effort to acquire a new identity. Others went through such anguish that they could not bring themselves to go out of the house. For such men to find a new identity, there is nothing as effective as love from a woman. A person realizes his identity only as someone else affirms it and builds it up for him. And it has to be someone that matters very much.

One needs to be quite a woman to put up with all the growing, however. "I think that women who marry priests have to be very strong," a priest's wife, Edna Berres, says. "Especially if the guy doesn't have a job, or is not financially secure. The women they marry have to be real supporters, not naggers. Allowing the guy to move from adolescence to adulthood in one easy year."

An Irishwoman, Maura Wall Murphy, observes that priests do in fact tend to marry strong women: "They always seem to choose independent, stronger women who have careers of their own or have a lot of interests. At first they are very dependent on the women, but as the years go by, that changes. The men grow up, the women are more cared for, and they love it. The men have settled down and have founded their own careers and no longer need to be so dependent.''

Many psychologists have wondered whether a person can mature at all without some kind of relationship with another person.[5] And while a relationship would not have to be sexual, there is no doubt that a healthy sexual relationship can be powerfully maturing. ''Sexuality matures you in other parts of your life,'' says a married priest, now a psychotherapist. ''The maturing goes far beyond sexuality, to responsibility in thinking about someone else, to sharing your life. I twice carried my wife, unconscious and bleeding to death, into the hospital (it was during those weeks after a birth). I carried my own son into the hospital after a seizure. The family is a new reality, expressed in a sexual relationship of man and woman. It creates a new social group, where feelings are a basis.''

This does not imply that men who leave are immature in every corner of their personality. They can be extremely mature in some ways; it is just that they can also have an imbalance in their growth. There are stages they have not yet gone through. They had been made to bypass much that had to do with their own sexual development; they have not passed through the socialization process of being with girls and young women *and* being free to associate, to experiment, to experience.

In particular, the naïveté that some priests bring to their sexual relationships could daunt many women. Usually, however, the physical side causes less trouble: The real problem is learning to relate intimately so long after late adolescence, when such learning should have taken place.

The adjustment to married life can be traumatic. Peter Beaman of Los Angeles went from a pastor's spacious rectory to a three-bedroom apartment containing a wife and five stepsons, aged from first grade to teens. ''I expected people to be deferential to me,'' he recalls. ''One of the boys really resented me—I had trained him to be an altar boy in the parish. It was very difficult for him to accept me as the priest who had trained him now replacing his father. We had a real falling out. Finally in one confrontation, he said, 'You were a wonderful priest—you're a rotten stepfather!' Of course he's accepted me long since.''

Shirley Ara of Los Angeles tells me she had to teach her husband, Charlie, what to do in a supermarket. ''And he was used to having people wait on him: Run-and-get-me-a-glass-of-water sort of thing.'' In the early days Charlie was shocked when people no longer volunteered to help with things like typing—they now expected to be paid for it. ''We priests' wives call it Bringing Up Father,'' Shirley says. ''We thought of writing a book about it.''

Yet most of these men do reach a healthy maturity. They can even recognize this new maturity in themselves. A common indication is that a man becomes a more careful driver. Here is a typical comment: ''I was a mad driver as a priest. I just didn't give a damn: I don't think I cared if I got killed. But now, with Helen and the kids, I just feel I've got to be more responsible.''

I know a number of priests who used to drink heavily, but now that they are married have no problems whatsoever with alcohol.

''Marriage has made me a better priest,'' explains a Spaniard who lives in Barcelona. ''When I was a priest, I was inclined to be an adventurer—with women, I mean. Now I am devoted to my wife and my family. I do not stray as I used to.''

A French priest told me that from his seminary days and all through his years as a missionary, he had been actively and indiscriminately homosexual: ''I lived a life that was totally selfish and irresponsible,'' he told me. ''But when I married, I resumed a normal heterosexual life. I have a son and two beautiful daughters now, and I've never looked back. My biggest regret is that I did not start heterosexual life earlier than I did: I could have had it in my twenties. I know I could have, because when I was at the lycée [high school] I dated girls, and girls were all I wanted.''

Most priests seem in the end to achieve mature and stable marriages. In Brazil, the resigned-priest organization Rumos gives a figure of 95 percent successful marriages. At a 1985 meeting with representatives of married-priest associations, the Vatican's Monsignor Canciani spoke of 10 percent of married priests divorcing. That indicates 90 percent of priestly marriages succeeding—a far higher figure than the secular norm for most countries.

However Terry Dosh, the national coordinator of the Corpus organization in America, questions this Vatican figure of 10 percent divorcing. ''How does the Vatican know such a percentage,'' he writes to me, ''when half the priests who marry don't even consult them? The two U.S. studies that I have seen put the figure under five percent—in fact one of them has two percent.''

Malcolm Muggeridge once said he would like to give Jesus Christ a tour of the Vatican and watch his reaction. I think I would like to take the pope on a tour of the married priests' homes that I have been in around the world. I doubt if it would change his views, but he would certainly see home after home where Christianity is lived and breathed.

Across the world I was astonished at families that begin the day with prayer around the breakfast table, families where the rosary survives and thrives, families that read the Bible daily, that pray together—parents and children—without the least embarrassment, families that manifest happiness, humor, social awareness, service, and what looks very like holiness.

There are no homes quite like the homes of married priests, and going from one to another around the world became for me a joyous pilgrimage. Nearly every time I was surprised and delighted. Whether the crucible of the early years refines, or whether love blooms in adversity, I am in no doubt that a priest's family life can be very good indeed.

"A good priest makes a good husband" is almost an axiom with priests' wives. Those wives who carry on about the impracticalities of their spouses often say that otherwise they make ideal partners. According to one Irish wife, "they seem to have a strongly developed anima [as opposed to animus, the macho, dominant, controlling part], so that there's a lot of feeling, creativity, and sensitivity. Having counseled many marriages, these men know the pitfalls. And they have learned compassion through counseling and hearing confessions."

One wife thinks priests make excellent parents "because they have a sense of fatherhood and the mystery of life. Maybe it's not that other men don't have these, but these guys can express them better, often in a very poetic way."

She says they are sensitive to women: "I watch them with their women. There's a respect there that you don't see with others—a caring. And I think their experience as confessors gives them a deep respect for confidences, a sensitivity. They become good listeners."

This wife, a professional counselor, guesses they make good sexual partners: "There's no way to measure how good they are as lovers, but they seem to be able to recognize their feelings and deal with them." She concedes there may be initial awkwardness on the physical side, "but dealing with feelings comes easier to them, so in the long term they have a better chance of a good relationship." Wives say these men show a noticeable concern with sexual giving as well as getting, treating them as "partners in joy, to be brought to arousal and fulfilled, rather than as objects of an exercise."

Some women regard their priest husbands as "fantastic lovers." Even if a man has led a totally celibate life, it seems that, after that initial adjustment, he is far from inhibited sexually. On the contrary, it is as though floodgates open and the wife finds herself carried along on torrents of physical passion and imaginative creativity that hardly seem to dwindle, even years into the marriage.

A Birmingham, England, wife finds priests more open in relationships: "They haven't been as hurt as young people through all the agonies of dating, so these men are less protective, less cautious. They are so free they can build up relationships without any double entendres."

"I'm often amazed at how fortunate priests are when they leave," says another wife. "They just come out, and within a year they have a fine girl. I think it is that women are so delighted to meet someone so up-front. With some other men in their thirties, there'd be questions—is he two-timing? Has he a mother problem? Is he gay? Is he AC/DC? Is he divorced or separated? Or is he just a bachelor who's protecting himself?"

In sum it would seem that being a priest makes a man a better husband, and being a husband makes him a better priest. Terry Dosh speaks of the process as "incarnational love." It takes time, he says, to arrive at the full insight of such love, "the profound experience of being human and hence limited; God as real through family; my wife as a sacrament; the birth of children as a sacrament; the preacher as a participant in life, not a coach on the sidelines. There is the sense that incarnational love makes us better priests and more dedicated to Christ, that one's wife reinforces my image of self as priest, and that having been so loved engenders the responsibility to love.

"Family union enhances ministry itself. Each loving act deepens one's sense of consecration; in a truly committed marriage, these occur very often—such as in caring for a sick wife or child; the many reconciliations daily. Many say family has given opportunities for involvement in community that they could not have had as celibate priests. Day-to-day problems create a clear and stronger focus on more incisive prayer life and a reality orientation."

These families of course are faced with the very same challenges that any other family immersed in today's culture is faced with. So it is not surprising that some married priests and their families appear to give in to the prevailing culture. I have not found many, but those I did find are sad. Priests who turn exclusively to big bucks and worldly success become haunted and driven men. However, for some of them the lurch toward Mammon is a temporary aberration. It is often due to feelings of insecurity at the time of their leaving, and to hearing people predict they "will never make it on the outside."

"When I was a priest," Mark Zwick of Houston told me, "we had stories of all the guys who left—stories of failure and slinging hash. After hearing those stories we had lots of anxiety about making it out there without the collar. Two years later there I am on the pavement, just left the ministry, with a wife and no job—a basket case."

A very few years later found Zwick as the head of the psychiatric emergency team for Stanislaus County, California. "I had a good position, money in the bank, two kids, two cars, a new house. Even the Church had more to do with me, because I had money." And Zwick loved it.

"But there was a Jewish lawyer in one of our groups, and he kept challenging us—what are you going to do next with your lives? It got to me. We're not by nature materialistic people, and I told my wife, this is silly—I don't see enough of the kids. I suggested we work half time and share the kids, and she got immediately into graduate school. But giving up the job was very hard: I could have been director of mental health for the whole of Stanislaus County. Then we decided to join Maryknoll as lay missionaries to be part of a team in Venezuela. But in the end we moved to El Salvador on our own steam, on the invitation of a priest there, who was then deported. . . ."

Mark and Louise Zwick now run the Casa Juan Diego in Houston, Texas—as a shelter and support house mostly for Hispanics and for illegal aliens. Mark has no salary at all. I have heard the couple compared to Mother Teresa.

Many priests who leave seem to go full circle and eventually arrive back at a balanced Christian life. As one married priest put it to me, "Somewhere along the line, we decided not to see the Church as the enemy. It's just ourselves, anyway."

However, one or both of the emotions, anger and guilt, can trouble some of these priests for a considerable time. The anger remains longest, at the institution, at the faceless ones, at former colleagues who turned their faces away. And since those colleagues too are often hurt and angry, as are those who administer the institution, what is sorely needed throughout the Catholic Church is reconciliation.

The guilt can be a torment to a married priest and doesn't need to have anything to do with rationality: I know priests who left for the clearest reasons, on the advice of superiors and with their blessing and encouragement, priests with full dispensations who have married in church, whose lives are an example of prayer and ministry—who nevertheless have suffered for some time an irrational guilt deep down in the gut.

It happened to me. In the early years of my marriage I would go through periods of anguish, where the whole center of my body, from solar plexus to groin, would tighten up and throb to my heartbeat. It might continue, without letup, for several weeks. It would usually be triggered off by something I had read, or something I might have heard on the news. I remember it hit me when Archbishop Romero was shot. If I rationalized it, I suppose I was telling myself that he died a martyr and I was still alive with a loving wife. But mostly it was just a physical feeling of awful anguish. At times the only thing that helped was a little prayer that hung from a banner in the Portland church where I was married: "Turn your face to me, O Lord, and give me peace." I would repeat it over and over, and it was like cool water reaching the hot coals deep in my belly.

Then one bright day the anguish would be completely gone, dissipated. I would have months and months free of it until some new thing would trigger it again.

The biggest mistake I made was not to confide in my wife—I did not want to lay my anguish on her, and did not want her to think I regretted leaving and marrying, which was far from the case. I would leave and marry all over again tomorrow without hesitation, because it was, and is, right for me. It was done with much prayer, and the encouragement and advice of respected colleagues and superiors.

A few years ago I confided in my wife what I used to suffer, and she said yes, she had known all along that there was something in me she could not reach and had longed for me to trust her with it.

I wish I had. She suffered more from my silence than if I had shared my suffering with her.

Curiously enough, the time I spent writing a novel helped me emerge from that suffering. The story was of a man who had done a killing in Ireland for political reasons, had fled to the United States, and there almost ruined his life through the guilt and anguish that dogged him for years. Into that man I projected my own anguish, and the very effort to describe it in detail was incredibly healing.

With the passing of years, the guilt faded into the light of common day. It had no basis in reality, and I am totally free of it now.

CHAPTER 6

The Gift Given Back?

I can never be thrown away. . . . In sickness, my sickness serves. . . . In perplexity, my perplexity may serve. . . . A preacher of truth in my own place.

Cardinal Newman

WHEN Pope John Paul II was in the United States in 1979 he made a heartfelt appeal to priests to remain faithful to their calling. "We do not return the gift once given," he cried. "It cannot be that God who gave the impulse to say yes, now wishes to hear no."

One priest, now married, pondered these words. "But I don't want to give back my priesthood," he told me. "It is possible to get more than one gift from a benevolent God. I have also received the gift of marriage—I am a man of all seven sacraments. Why can't I use both priesthood and marriage for the glory of God?"

Does that mean that he would come running back into Church employment if the celibacy rule changed? It does not. I have met few resigned priests who simply want to return to an unchanged clerical institution. A great many, however, feel a strong urge to serve others, to act out Christ's words, "I was sick and you visited me; I was hungry and you gave me to eat." In that sense there is a very clear drive toward ministry, and it has led in fact to many kinds of ministry being practiced. But it hasn't a great deal to do with the ecclesiastical system.

"I'm a church rat," says Frank Bonnike of Chicago. "It's in me." When Frank left to marry, he considered a career in business but very soon realized ministry was his vocation and always would be. For nine years after he left, Frank was a general-duty chaplain in a large Lutheran hospital. "I was simply a chaplain who happened to be a Catholic," he says. That meant counseling, being with the sick and dying, caring for the bereaved. "On occasion, of course, I baptized, heard confessions, or anointed, but only when necessary and always according to the Church's laws [in cases of necessity]." He told me the late Cardinal Cody once promised him he would never try to get him fired from his chaplaincy work.

Bonnike is now involved in prison ministry and is the administrator of PACE, an organization that works to rehabilitate ex-prisoners.

Most priests who leave feel themselves lovingly pursued by the Hound of Heaven and could not shake off their priesthood even if they would. As Terry Dosh puts it: "The spiritual legacy that married priests continue to have after resignation calls for service to God and others. This can be exercised in many ways, but MUST be exercised. Those who do not, end up with some psychological, social, emotional or physical consequences. . . . One cannot deny a legacy without severe consequences.[1]

But that does not mean going back into the system. Given optional celibacy, some *might* perhaps consider reentering, but with their wives and families—a survey done in Spain indicates 23 percent, and Corpus in the United States suggests up to one third.[2] However, invariably such priests say they first would want to see very significant changes in Church structures. "I'd want to renegotiate my way in," says one Irish priest. "I'd want to work out something I could give meaning to, not simply go back and take up passively where I left off."

"Going back in would be a terrible regression," a Seattle priest believes. "Could I in good conscience give the party line on *Humanae Vitae* [the birth-control encyclical]? It was a monkey on my back when I was a priest, and fifteen years later I'm still picking up walking wounded from that encyclical. And what they did to [Archbishop] Hunthausen was an absolute travesty. Do I want to be part of an institution that does that to people? On the other hand, maybe if I were inside I could cushion the blow for people.''

"I left because the Church didn't know how to use us," says a German priest. "If it couldn't use us then, how can it use us now?"

An Irish priest puts it in Irish terms: "Do you think I want to go back to living over the shop, to *Humanae Vitae*, to no girl altar boys, to the pope's notion of women, to taking money for masses, to being a dispensing machine for sacraments, to blessing water with relics, to total control taken over my life and now over my wife's, to being a full-frontal cleric [wearing blacks and collar]? Not for all the tea in China. I just want to put something back into the people of God, who ultimately put up the money for training me. They used to tell us the pennies of the poor supported us: Well, now I work for the poor.''

Cardinal Lorscheider says it more gently, in more Brazilian terms: "Married priests are not so much interested in celebrating mass, but in asking themselves how can we, trained as priests, yet today part of the laity, how can we use our gift in this world? They are more interested in their own responsibilities in society. It is so different here from in Europe, where there is more a spirit of confrontation about ministry.''

I distinguish four different kinds of ministry among priests who have left. The first is the ministry on which Christ said He would judge all of us—"I was hungry and you gave me to eat. . . . I was naked and you clothed me"—the ministry we are all required to do from our baptism. The second involves giving the sacraments when necessary, even though outside formal Church structures. The third is voluntary part-time ministry in the official Church. And the fourth is a return to full-time Church employment, to which married priests are being recalled to a considerable degree in many parts of the world.

THE WORKS OF MERCY

"Evert, waarom moest je weg" ("Why did you have to leave")? These are the words of Fr. Gregory Brenninkmeijer, a provincial of the Dutch Jesuits, talking to the ex-Jesuit Evert Verheijden. "What you are doing now, Evert, is all pure Jesuit work

and priestly work.'' Evert told me they both got so emotional that they could not continue for a few minutes.

Brenninkmeijer is right. Evert is doing the same lecturing, counseling, and caring that he always did. The only difference is that he comes home to his wife, Else, after work. The Verheijdens are approaching seventy and have come a long way from that day many years ago that Jesuit Evert became physically completely paralyzed. ''The doctors found it was psychosomatic: I did not know where to go anymore—in society, in the Church, in the priesthood.'' The paralysis gradually lifted as Evert worked toward a decision to leave. And twenty years later Evert is a dynamo of energy. He is fulfilled, and his energy and happiness spill over into his counseling.

All over the world I find married and resigned priests continuing the works of mercy to which they had given their lives. There is, for example, Edward Kelly of Sapang Palay in the Philippines. In the early sixties, Fr. Kelly was a newly arrived Irish missionary when twenty-five thousand squatters were forcibly uprooted from Manila. They and their dismantled scrap-wood shacks were dumped thirty miles out in the middle of a wilderness that lacked roads, sewerage, anything. The people simply sank into despair, drunkenness, dreariness, and drugs.

Young Fr. Kelly volunteered to join them, without knowing the language, with no plans, with no training in community development. He just arrived, and as he says today, ''God did the rest.'' He started a tiny school. He organized a march on the palace of President Marcos, a march that brought bulldozers and graders to build the promised streets in Sapang Palay.

The school grew, was destroyed by a typhoon, and grew again. Then Ed Kelly and the people started a high school. Eventually, after years of growing and developing, they had the temerity to start a third-level college. And all the time organizing the building of first, 250 houses, then 400 more, the 400 more . . . and more and more, for an area growing to one hundred thousand from continued forcible relocations.

Today Sapang Palay has those schools, as well as prenursery and nursery schools and kindergarten, three big libraries, a large farm to train locals in vegetable gardening, a medical team with several clinics, Christ the King Church and several chapels, a five-person guidance team, a six-person religious instruction and

Christian-living team, and free tuition for members of large families and for the poor.

It is not really Ed Kelly who has done all this—it is the people themselves, whom Ed convinced they had it within themselves to do. The most important thing constructed in Sapang Palay is the vibrant, self-confident community that thrives there today.

In 1982, with hardly a ripple, Fr. Ed Kelly married within the community he had served for eighteen years and has simply gone on with his work in Sapang Palay.

People were delighted he married a local girl (she was back home after graduating from Manila University). As one old woman expressed it, "By marrying Minda you've turned your back on your own country and you've become one of us." Recently Ed wrote a book that reveals that before he met his wife, he had gone through years of loneliness so desperate that it had almost driven him out of his mind.[3]

Today he continues his missionary work, his inspiring of the local community, the direction of Assumption College, and his unremitting dedication to the poor of Sapang Palay, who see him as one of themselves. The two differences in his life are that he now has a vigorous young wife to back him in his work and he may no longer celebrate mass—a great grief to him. And there is a third difference: He and Minda have a couple of lovely children.

A significant number of priests when they leave deliberately opt for careers that are in fact a form of ministry. Two married priests, Dennis Dooley and Stanley Gofron, are both adult probation officers in Texas, dealing daily with convicted criminals. John Flavin is a program coordinator in the Southwest for AIDS education and risk education. In Cartagena, Colombia, Hugo Aceros and his wife, Leonor, have devoted the eighteen years since their marriage to the creation of an agricultural co-op and to the education of the campesinos in a village of the interior. Jim Shannon, once the auxiliary bishop of St. Paul-Minneapolis and now a vice president of General Mills in charge of funding, has as his ministry the disbursement of over $8 million annually. Even more of a ministry is his immense personal influence for good in Minnesota public affairs, a greater one than he ever had as a bishop. And he was recently described as "one of the outstanding people in philanthropy in America."

In the same city the former Dominican Joe Selvaggio devotes

his life to employing the hard-to-employ and developing housing for the disadvantaged, especially underprivileged Native Americans. "He's a moral force," remarks the local police chief. "Jesus told us clothe the naked and house the homeless," Joe says. Project for Pride in Living (PPL), which he founded and has continued with the help of three other married priests, builds sixty new housing units a year and refurbishes dozens of old houses. It also runs a light-manufacturing plant, employing people no one else wants. "The aim is to give people back their dignity," Joe states.

According to Dr. Terry Dosh, over 60 percent of priests who leave take jobs in some sort of social services—as teachers, psychotherapists, social workers, counselors. One could argue that some simply choose a role close to the caring ministry they already knew. It is interesting, however, how many others who are in purely commercial or administrative jobs nevertheless seek out ministry during their free time.

A psychologist, Don Conroy, believes that many priests who left—himself included—were conditioned by their experience as priests and, after leaving, proceeded to obtain further training, education, and certification to act as professionals. Thereby they were able to distinguish for the first time between their social role or profession and their personal life. To make this distinction is a step toward maturity.

Bob Boler, a former Maryknoll missionary in Japan and now an Arizona state official, spends much of his free time ministering to the dying. The local pastor has encouraged him, and lately Bob's three teenage daughters have started to accompany him.

Rana Boler, his seventeen-year-old daughter, says: "One time sticks in my mind. Uncle Lee (he was really an in-law) had liver cancer. Dad helped him a lot: He was the only person there to do what was to be done. I was around all the time: We actually saw him die. It was our first death experience. I was scared, really sad. But I also felt really comforted, especially since it was the first time I really saw my father cry. We went back the next morning. Dad said, 'He's at peace,' and he took my hand and just put it on Uncle Lee's. 'Say good-bye,' Dad said. He really made it easier."

Rakel Boler, age fifteen, says: "It may sound kinda funny, but this is something we want to do. We're just normal teenagers, but it's the way Dad raised us—to help and comfort others. It's just born in us. It's not a chore: It just seems right."

SACRAMENTAL MINISTRY

One night in Recife, Brazil, I went with the married priest Brian Eyre to sit in on the regular Wednesday meeting of dwellers in a *favela*. These people have formed a little neighborhood group which they call a "base community." We drove over dirt tracks swarming with children and dogs, passed makeshift open-air shops with bare-chested men, bumped across a concrete slab ("covers the sewer pipes we put in," Eyre said).

They were handsome people gathered in the tiny hall, mostly black, neatly dressed, and in that sultry night atmosphere there was the smell of soaped, clean bodies. A fluorescent light lit the little hall and a fan whirred ("the electricity we brought in," whispered Eyre). I found myself thinking, I'm sitting here watching a married priest who got all this going only five years ago, and you'd hardly notice him, except for the pink skin. He's just one of the group.

One reason Brian Eyre is so accepted is that, like St. Paul the tentmaker, he works for his living. He teaches English. "I see no obstacle between having a job and doing pastoral work," Brian says. "I could earn more than I do, but my boss knows that on two nights a week I work in the *favela*. That's a decision Marta and I came to."

What does he do in the *favela?* "Exactly what I used to do when I was a pastor," he says. "Most of my work then was with the poorest—it was raising their consciousness, their awareness, reflecting with them on their reality of no water, no sewerage, health problems, garbage, rats. . . . But reflecting in the light of what it says in the Gospels. Now they've reached the stage where they have leaders that can go to the prefecture and demand garbage collections and rat control."

Why does he bother with all this? "Because I'm happy doing it. This is what makes me tick. And Marta has reinforced this ticking—she was a nun. She hasn't in any way made me tick less."

Like so many other married priests, Brian Eyre has been careful not to intrude on the sacramental area reserved to celibate priests, particularly as he got word that the new ultraconservative bishop (the replacement of Helder Camara) had expressly sent word that Eyre was to have no liturgical function whatsoever in church. But something happened lately to make Brian Eyre wonder about this:

"We moved recently, and we live now where no priest ever

sets foot. It's abandoned. There's only myself and Marta—they call her *a mulher do padre* ("the priest's wife"). Well, there was a woman here 101 years old—born the year before slavery ended in Brazil. The people came to tell me she was dying and asked me to come. With the community we tried to improve her physical necessities. That done, I said to the people, let's pray. We prayed. To me, what we did was the sacrament of the sick: The Church was present there.

"A week later there was a knock on the door. They told us she was dead, and the people asked if I would do the funeral service. So while the bishop said I can't have service, the people came and asked me. I actually got a call from the People of God. I didn't ask them: They came and asked me."

When I left Recife, Brian Eyre was still pondering his dilemma. People are starting to ask more of him. He wants to obey the Church, but the Vatican Council says explicitly that the Church *is the People of God*—those same people of God that summoned him to serve them. It is clear that they will be asking more and more of him soon in the matter of the sacraments. What answer should Brian Eyre give to them? Is he to say yes or no to the People of God? To the Church?

All over the world I am finding this phenomenon—where the people are calling their married priests back to sacramental service.

Some of these priests still feel they must say no. A Colombian married priest described his anguish to me: "We have so many abandoned towns, towns that don't have priests. It would be beautiful if, in such places, one of us could go there, preach, say mass, in places like Santa Rosa. We are actually invited by the people, but we say we can't because the bishop won't permit it. They say they don't understand the Church. . . . If they only knew it—they are the Church. But there was one resigned married priest in the Magdalena region who did do it—did the mass and the sacraments for the people, and went to jail for it. He was accused of usurping the powers of the clergy."

Others, however, are beginning to say yes, as in Madrid, where Julio Perez Pinillos, the animator of Spain's married-priest group, explicitly declares, "If a concrete existing community sends and asks us for the celebration of mass and the sacraments, we simply do not have the right to refuse them."

It is happening all over the world—American resigned priests working in hospitals are regularly called on to hear confessions and administer the sacrament of the sick (and for those in danger of death are authorized by Church law do so); in one midwest small town, when the alcoholic pastor refuses to do baptisms, the people take their children to a nearby married priest; and in Holland, France, Germany, and Ireland, I have encountered or heard of people turning to married, resigned, or suspended priests and asking them for mass, baptisms, weddings, and the sacrament of the sick.

Events particularly in Latin America indicate that local communities are sensing they have a right to mass and the sacraments, and that they have a right to select someone to minister to them, and to call upon that person to do so. While it seems to arise from a sort of community instinct, theologians of high standing, such as Edward Schillebeeckx, hold that communities should be able to choose and call their ministers. In his book *Ministry,* Schillebeeckx suggests too that changes in the Church can come from the bottom upward: "From the history of the church it seems that there is a way in which Christians can develop a practice in the church from below, from the grass-roots, which for a time can compete with the official practice recognized by the church, and which in its Christian opposition and illegality can eventually nevertheless become the dominant practice of the church, and finally be sanctioned by the official church."[4]

VOLUNTARY CHURCHWORK

In 1987 I spent some time in west London, England. For Sunday morning mass friends took me, not to the large and institutional parish church on the high street, but to a little community center, dwarfed by battered and fearsome high rises.

In that community center everybody knew everybody. Children romped among the chairs and the trestle tables where coffee and homemade buns were being laid out. There were black families, Irish families, Filipinos, and real Londoners of the old stock. Maybe eighty or one hundred people all told.

The priest's short talk really meant something to me, and I felt quite moved when he publicly welcomed me, and people turned around to smile and take my hand. It really was a sign of peace.

This is as close to being a base community as I have found

anywhere in the world. It is having an impact. You can see it in the
faces: These people are not lonely, not sour, not frustrated. They
enjoy being there, and they relish the good news they hear there.
There is far more to it than just being at weekly mass: This is a
community that looks after its members, who are in regular contact
throughout the week—a community that also reaches out to the
many Asian and non-Christian groups in the area.

In this particular part of London people remark on a distinct
sense of community. This little Catholic base community is only
one of many forces for good, but its effects are felt and noticed. And
remarked on.

Among the small group of committed Catholic laypeople responsible for building this community spirit, I frequently heard
mention of Luis and Margaret Ulloa. They are a married couple who
seem to work closely and effectively with the local Catholic priests.
Luis is from Ecuador, and Margaret is London-born and bred. What
people did not mention, however, was that Luis Ulloa is a priest
who resigned and married. I'm not sure if people were even aware
of it, or if it simply did not matter.

I went to see Luis and Margaret Ulloa. It was clear that they
saw what they did as a normal part of life for a married priest and
his wife still dedicated to ministry. They are but one instance of a
worldwide phenomenon, where priests who left are being drawn
back into involvement with their local church on a voluntary basis.
Sometimes they offer their services; sometimes the local pastor
comes looking for them.

In many parts of the world there are now active pastors who are
totally committed to involving their married ex-colleagues as far as
possible in the life of the Church—pastors such as Fr. Frank Zap-
atelli of Phoenix, Arizona, or Fr. Joe Kramis of Federal Way, near
Seattle, who has six married priests in the parish and has managed
to get them all involved with his church. It is not a matter of mass
or the sacraments, but of the myriad other tasks and ministries a
well-run church community demands.

In Lima, Peru, former missionary David Molyneux took his
family to live in a new parish, presided over by an old Belgian priest
who had sixty thousand people to care for. Molyneux presented
himself to the priest and offered his services. The old man fell on his
shoulders: "Just what I need, dear brother. Could you do the seven
o'clock mass on Sunday?"

"Now, not so fast, Father," Molyneux said. "You see, I've left, I'm married, and I've got kids."

"Oh." The old man's jaw dropped. "I, uh, I don't know what anyone would think of my having a former priest working here." Then he brightened up. "Tell you what—come with me to one of my areas and I'll introduce you around. We'll take it from there."

Dave started going regularly to that area, sitting in at meetings, participating in the community, getting involved with education for the youngsters. "They really want me there now," he told me. "They realize I have something to offer. I find I have risen to a position of leadership. The auxiliary bishop comes up now and then: He knows me from the past and has no problem with it."

By way of contrast, a married priest, Bernie Groom, returned to Ireland and settled in the town of Kinnegad. He offered his services to the local parish priest to help in giving out communion.

"Well now, I don't think we're supposed to do that," said the pastor. And that was the end of that.

The pastor of course was referring to the various provisos that the Vatican still attaches to dispensations, which attempt to exclude dispensed priests from any liturgical function whatsoever in Church. However Cardinal Lorscheider told me he believes those rules should be interpreted in the light of the more tolerant statements from the 1971 Bishops' Synod and from the bishops' meeting in Puebla.

Much, of course, depends on the attitude of the pastor. Pastors have been known to treat offers of help with contempt ("You can clean up the church grounds," said one), whereas others are glad to put every function they can within the reach of the married priest. There is a dilemma for a married priest who is offered work that seems humiliating or demeaning—should he insist on nothing short of real priestly ministry, thus stressing the reality of his priesthood, or should he show Christian humility and accept whatever crumbs of ministry are thrown to him?

In spite of Vatican prohibitions, bishops too are starting to reach out to their priests, and you find married and resigned priests serving voluntarily on diocesan committees, acting as consultants to a diocese (if they have perhaps become specialists in psychology or finance), doing adult religious education, and giving retreats. Bernie Henry, a married priest in Chicago, serves on Cardinal Bernardin's personnel board and is a member of the Association of

Chicago Priests. In San Diego, Paul Dion teaches adult religious education for the diocese and sits on the diocesan marriage annulment tribunal.

CHURCH EMPLOYMENT

My first sight of Matt Purcell was on a Sunday morning, after lurching over miles of Brazil's red clay tracks with *favelas* on every side, some just clusters of hovels made from flattened oil drums and plywood, others mutating into concrete-block settlements. My driver was a priest from the diocese. Finally we stopped at what looked like a small garage with the doors open wide, and there was a crowd clustered around the doors. A smiling Brazilian woman in her thirties greeted us, rocking a baby carriage with infant twins, and holding by the hand a blonde two-year-old girl who glared suspiciously up at us. "Matt Purcell's wife," my companion said. "Used to be a nun."

She handed over the carriage to a nearby child and led us through the little crowd to the top end of the garage. At a makeshift altar, a slender fair-haired young man with a face of quite unusual serenity was just ending a quiet-spoken homily in Portuguese. He wore an open-necked shirt and gray slacks, and a priest's narrow white stole hung from his shoulders. He came over and shook hands with us, then went on with the mass. Suddenly we were saying the Our Father together and then it was communion time, and I realized there had been no consecration. This was a communion service.

I stayed a week with Matt Purcell and his wife, Sandra. Sitting in their tiny kitchen, I found the whole notion of compulsory celibacy shot to ribbons. Fearsome-looking mustachioed men came in to drink coffee with Matt, and women and wives dropped in and out to talk with Sandra.

"There's a place for a woman in all this," Matt explained to me, "where a man can't go. They ask Sandra about problems they would never have brought to me in confession. And they tell her about a lot of things they would never tell me."

The Purcells live in utter simplicity on a tiny income partly from the bishop and partly from the Irish missionary order to which Matt was once attached. It's not a terribly secure existence, but

Purcell says you have to take risks and have faith in God. "You do worry, but if you opt out of the system, nothing will ever change. The thing is to stay and make a space for what you are doing. You get more and more accepted. You keep working with these groups— after a while they forget you are married."

Does the bishop forget it?

"He put us in here. If he could have married clergy in the morning, he would have. A fair number of bishops here would do so, but there's no way they can go against Rome.

"Many of the Brazilian celibate priests here have women on the side anyway. You see, any sort of social life is impossible— forget about golf or anything like that—so priests would have to live like hermits. And anyway, people don't believe any priest is celibate."

Matt says that even with a wife and family, the work itself can be lonely and sometimes heartbreaking. "It's good when someone like you comes to visit. When a man has been here a while, you get so caught up in the whole question of rights for people, the whole distribution of wealth problem. Do you know that a thousand babies die of malnutrition every day in this country? That's the yearly equivalent of five Hiroshima bombs. Did you ever hear of infants tearing their mother's dress looking for milk?"

What ministry do Matt and Sandra do? Their nonsacramental work consists in bringing people to an awareness that the Gospel does not want acceptance and resignation, but that in the light of that Gospel they can change things. And the sacramental ministry includes everything a celibate priest does—baptisms, weddings, anointings, funerals, blessings, preaching, retreats—everything, in fact, except the words of consecration at mass and the words of absolution in confession.

And why not those words? "That's because I'm married," Matt says with a wry grin.

The nonsense implied in such a ruling should become more evident as more and more married priests like Matt Purcell come back into church service and have to tiptoe around the words of consecration and absolution, just because they love a wife. In that one area of the city, there are eight other married priests now back in the diocese, running churches, chapels, and parishes. When I went to see the auxiliary bishop who had brought them all back, I found a man who combined courage and subtlety.

"My overriding principle," he told me cannily, "is, whatever a lay minister can do, a married priest can do. Now a lay minister can be a minister of baptism, can witness marriages, can be the animator of a community, can instruct in religion, can be a special minister for the Eucharist. I don't go beyond that. And a final affirmation to justify this is Church law—the very final article in the Code of Canon Law is this: *In ecclesia, suprema lex, salus animarum* ['In the church, the supreme law is the salvation of souls'].[5]

"We have to give a reply to the people when they look for priests. We have an immense country, where the majority is Catholic and is abandoned, without pastors. My own region has three million people. What I do, I do with tranquility, as a successor of the Apostles, and because of my pastoral responsibility.

"Nobody has the competence to prevent what we do here. I have no right to prohibit the exercise of that part of a man's priesthood that comes from his baptism. Because that mandate he gets directly from Christ—his baptism inserts him into the community, and he has a duty to serve it.

"I believe that married men must be ordained priests, and I think it is a matter of urgency. Much more important than tying celibacy and priesthood together is to guarantee to the people that they'll have a priest, married or not."

There is one married priest I can identify, because he is already well known. Bern Brown is the pastor of Our Lady of the Snows Mission in Colville, which is in Canada's Northwest Territories. As a young oblate missionary, he single-handedly founded and built the mission at Colville Lake, fifty miles above the Arctic Circle, where he had found a small group of Indians called the "End of the Earth People." It has grown into a settlement of sixty-five, with its own airstrip and accommodation for sportfishermen, where Bern has at various times hosted Prime Minister Trudeau as well as Prince Charles.

In 1971 Bern was dispensed from celibacy and married Margaret, an Eskimo girl who was a former cross-country skiing record holder. His bishop flew up to do the wedding in the little log church. However, Bern still carries on as pastor, except that he may not celebrate mass. A missionary from Fort Good Espe flies in once a month to perform that duty.

Bern also carries on as the community doctor, dentist, secretary of the co-op, manager of the fishing lodge, and curator of the

Indian museum he founded. He has become a well-known painter and flies his own Cessna ninety miles south every week for the mail. There is no other way to reach Colville.

In some places the wheel has turned almost full circle, and priests who left and married years ago are finding themselves called back into Church work. In the United States the Corpus organization publishes a list of the various ministries now performed by such priests. Some are voluntary, and some are full-time paid occupations. Ministries of worship are first listed:

1. Minister for communion service, with readings, preaching and prayers, when no [celibate] priest is available for daily or Sunday mass.

2. Preacher on occasion, either following the Gospel proclamation or at a later point in the liturgy.

3. Eucharistic minister (communion to the sick and shut-ins).

4. Lector; commentator; liturgical planner.

5. Music minister; cantor; song leader.

6. Minister for prayers and blessings at wakes, funerals, burials.

7. Minister for anointing of the sick, and sacrament of Reconciliation in emergencies.

Married priests also perform the following pastoral ministries:

1. Administrator of a parish with a resident pastor.

2. Administrator of a parish without a resident pastor.

3. University campus minister.

4. Hospital chaplain; director of pastoral care.

5. Secretary to bishop.

6. Chancellor of diocese.

7. Director of religious education on diocesan and parish levels. Religious education teacher.

8. Director of diocesan Family Life Bureau.

9. Diocesan director of social services; director of Catholic charities.

10. Diocesan ecumenical commission, and preaching in other Christian churches.

11.   Director of specialized ministries: youth; mentally and physically handicapped; alcohol- and drug-rehabilitation; the elderly; hospice for dying.

12.   Principal of Catholic elementary or high school; diocesan director of education.

13.   Director of diocesan Justice and Peace Office.

14.   Diocesan psychologist.

15.   Director of parish catechumenate programmes.

16.   Parish adult education, advent and lenten programmes.

17.   Parish counsellor; diocesan counseling service.

18.   Director of preparation programmes for parish infant baptism, confirmation, marriage.

19.   Retreat master; director of days of recollection.

20.   Lecturer at clergy conferences; moderator of priest-support groups.

21.   Theology professor in Catholic colleges and universities.[6]

It is clear that many of these functions are in direct contradiction to the Vatican's instructions on laicized priests, which appear to be more and more ignored around the world, even by bishops. Not everyone, however, even among the married priests, sees it as a step forward that some should now be returning to full-time church employment. It can have its drawbacks.

If for example, a man left to get away from clerical control and domination of his life, by again taking up paid church employment he would be walking right back into the same situation again. But this time he would be far more vulnerable—first, because he would have a family dependent on him, and second, because he could now be fired on the employer's whim, which could not happen to a celibate priest. It would be naïve to think that certain Church authorities would have grown mellower with the years, especially if they had even more economic power over a man than they had before.

A member of Britain's Advent group of married priests pointed out to me that some of its members keep a low profile and make no attempt to shift public opinion on married priests, simply because they are employed as teachers in Catholic schools. They have to keep their heads down if they want to keep their jobs.

A married priest employed by the Church of today would be

haunted by insecurity. He is dependent on goodwill, not on established rights or employment practices. Even if the employer, whether a priest or bishop, is a man of conviction and generosity, he must eventually resign or die and could be replaced by a pharaoh who knew not Joseph. There are no guarantees of similarly fair treatment by the successor.

Some resigned priests who have gone back to work for the Church have spoken of low pay, stigma, humiliation, and of being treated with coldness, hostility, or envy by celibate colleagues.

There is also the danger of exploitation. In a large parish on the East Coast, a married priest has been taken on as assistant to the pastor. The pastor happens to be a lazy man who plays golf all the time and has simply dumped the whole work of the parish—bar the words of consecration and absolution—on the shoulders of his poorly paid married assistant. This man has an enormous load which includes answering sick calls to several nearby hospitals. With work extending to all hours of day and night, hardly any time off, and no help from his pastor, the man's home life is suffering, and his wife is growing angry.

Lastly, there is a feeling in some quarters that returning to full Church work, on less than equal terms, postpones rather than hastens the day when celibacy will become optional, when married priests will have equal place and status with their celibate colleagues.

As yet it is an unresolved issue and one that is getting more and more consideration among married priests as more and more are invited back.

There is, however, no discussion, or any need for it, on the primary role of the married and resigned priest in the Church today. To echo the words of St. Theresa of Lisieux, it is to do the ordinary things extraordinarily well so that the world will look at these men and their families and say, "See how these Christians love one another." As Carole Hegarty of Chicago puts it: "Preaching was never any good without example. Now they only have example."

Don Franzoni, the former abbot of St. Paul's Outside-the-Walls, was asked what message he had for resigned priests. "Tell them this," he said. "Not from me, but from St. Paul. Who can separate us from the love of Christ Jesus? Neither sword nor death, nor suffering nor exile."

Don Franzoni believes that a resigned priest still has two duties—"the first is to continue a dialogue with the Church so it becomes a church of service, not of power. Remember the center of the Church is not Rome, but Christ. And the second duty is to continue to meet the needs of men and to preach the gospel.

"Even if laicized," Don Franzoni says, "I am still responsible for the word of God. Woe to me if I do not preach the gospel, as St. Paul said. Remember that even canon law gives me the right and duty to minister to someone at the point of death. Well, I have a similar duty to the living. If I meet a young person without hope, I have the same duty to give him the gospel."

CHAPTER 7

Priests Who Stay

Christ's lore and his Apostles twelve he taught,
But first he followed it himself.

Chaucer, The Canterbury Tales

A few years ago a professional killer was hired to assassinate Dom Helder Camara, the archbishop of Recife-Olinda in Brazil. He was paid by certain of the country's powerful landowners who felt threatened from the way Dom Helder was raising the consciousness of Brazil's millions of poor.

Dom Helder lives in a little house with a walled garden in front, and a door in the wall leading to the street. The man rang the bell at the door and a frail five-foot man of seventy-nine came out to open it. The visitor asked to see Dom Helder.

"That's me," said the little man.

"*You* are Dom Helder?" stammered the assassin, his image of the evil "Communist" bishop immediately shattered.

The archbishop led his guest through the little garden into the house and gave him a chair. "Now," he said. "What can I do to help you?"

"Nothing," the man said, his hand trembling. "I don't want to have anything to do with you, because you are not the sort of person I could kill."

"Kill? But why do you want to kill?" asked Dom Helder.

"I was paid to kill you," was the answer. "But I can't do it."

"If you've been paid, why don't you do it?" said Dom Helder reasonably. "I will go to the Lord."

"No," the man said. "You are one of the Lord's." He got up and went away.[1]

Some years later, after I passed through that same garden to spend an hour with Dom Helder, I understood what the assassin had meant. Dom Helder Camara is one of the Lord's. By which I mean that the Lord has clearly answered his most frequent prayer, borrowed from Cardinal Newman: "Lord Jesus, do not extinguish the light of your presence within me. O Lord, look through my eyes, speak through my lips, walk with my feet. Lord, may my poor human presence be a reminder, however weak, of your divine presence."

Dom Helder Camara is a priest who stayed, and he could be a symbol of many other priests who have stayed and truly lived their celibacy and have grown in wisdom and grace before God and men.

One cannot of course assert that all priests stay for the right motives, and it is clear that not all grow within the priesthood. But many do. And there is nothing quite like a priest who has stayed and truly grown in his priesthood, or is striving to do so. "Since I left," an Irish married priest told me, "I've known groups of teachers, media people, every kind. But the men I knew in the priesthood, I'd still rate those men as above all the groups I've known since I left."

If this book is to speak of men who have left the ministry and are still striving to grow in God's love, it would be inaccurate if it failed to salute those who, without ever leaving, have been striving thus all their lives.

The great French Dominican, Henri Lacordaire, summed up the ideal of the celibate priesthood in a memorable passage: "To live in the midst of the world, with no desire for its pleasures; to be a member of every family, yet belonging to none; to share all sufferings, to penetrate all secrets, to heal all wounds; to go daily from men to God, to offer Him their homage and petitions, to return from God to men, to bring them His pardon and His hope; to have a heart of iron for chastity and a heart of flesh for charity; to teach and to pardon, console and bless and to be blessed forever. O God, what a life is this, and it is thine, O priest of Jesus Christ."

It is an ideal that has grown progressively harder to strive for as the traditional supports for celibate priesthood have been steadily eroded in modern pluralist society.

It can take something akin to heroism to live celibacy well—when the world no longer believes in celibacy or that any man could be really celibate; when the wrongdoings of other celibate priests tarnish the image of all priesthood; when a man feels betrayed by colleagues who leave; when thousands of former colleagues seem fulfilled and happily married; when the priest himself believes celibacy should be optional; when overwork and stress is overwhelming due to the growing scarcity of priests; when authority treats priests like pawns; when the comforts of the world seduce through television; when Church authorities seem to be turning their backs on the promise of the Vatican Council.

Yet some priests do not merely endure but grow through all of this. They are men of resurrection and I have been privileged to know a few. There was my uncle, the Dominican Fr. Oliver Gabriel Stokes. I became a priest because of his example and years later he did my wedding. When he died in 1983, he was a friend more than an uncle. A man with enough personality quirks to make him thoroughly human, and with enough humor to keep the Dominican Order chuckling for half a century, he made giving—of himself and the little he possessed—as vital as breathing.

He spent years as a missionary in Trinidad, and when he used to depart for Europe on leave, the people of the parish would charter buses to come to the docks or the airport to see him off. I am told people in Trinidad still talk about him, a quarter of a century after he left for the last time. At his funeral, other priests were seen weeping, which a very old priest told me is the rarest of tributes from one priest to another.

My very last memory is of him sitting up in his hospital bed, with a glass of Jameson's Irish whiskey in his hand, three hours before he died. Around the bed were two young Dominican seminarians who were his friends, and myself.

"Did y'ever hear," said my uncle, "of the two fellas coming out of the pub? 'Better let me drive, Michael,' one says to the other. ' 'Cause you're too drunk.'

" 'Whaddaya mean, I'm too drunk? It's my car, and I'm driving!'

"Well, they lurched along for about an hour. Then Frank says, 'You must be getting near a town now, Michael.'

" 'Why so?'

" ' 'Cause you're knocking down more people.'
" 'Whaddaya mean, I'm knocking them down? I thought you were doing the driving!' "

Those were practically my uncle's last words to me. He died in his sleep later that night, at the age of seventy-four. I think maybe he died chuckling.

Then there was Paul Hynes, another Dominican, and the closest friend I ever had in the world. We joined the Dominicans the same day, detested each other on sight, and fought like cats for two years. Then, inexplicably, we became friends for life. On one vacation after ordination we explored Europe with a motorcycle and tent. People wondered how we could even stand each other, as Paul was Teutonically efficient, and I was—not.

I watched Paul Hynes grow from an impatient, somewhat arrogant youngster, through an efficient and still impatient administrator, to a priest in his forties who combined strength, sensitivity, and love in a way that few could have predicted. He had a zeal to spread God's word, and a quite extraordinary concern for others, even in the midst of the wasting illness he had.

After I left the ministry, he remained my closest friend. He remained genuinely celibate too—I know, because he told me so. He would be in his fifties now had he lived, but that terrible wasting illness took him.

For a while after he died, I used to pray for him. Lately I find myself praying *to* him.

On visits to London I kept hearing so much about Fr. Michael Hollings, a parish priest in Bayswater, that I went and visited him. In writing this book, I decided to let him speak for the many other devoted and generous celibate priests who still grace the Church.

Michael Hollings was a young Guards officer in World War II. He had a girlfriend, lots of personality, and no religious faith whatsoever. Somehow or other he became a believer and then told the chaplain he wanted to be a priest.

"But you don't even go to church," spluttered the chaplain. "How could you want to say mass?"

"I want to help people," said young Hollings.

"Well, be a social worker then!"

"No. I want to be a priest."

Michael Hollings has been a priest for many years now—he

must be touching seventy. He appears to be a very happy man. Wherever he becomes pastor he practices his notorious "open-door" policy, and there gradually accumulates in the parish rectory a sort of impromptu floating community. There is also tea and sandwiches twice a day at the church door for all the poor in the district. And at the time of this writing, seventeen people are "in residence" in the Bayswater rectory: a West Indian, who plays the guitar and studies accounting; Old Sister Joe in her eighties; a Coptic Ethiopian; Emily, twenty-one, who is studying the organ; a nun from Dublin; somebody named Antoinette; a man who tried to become a priest, and wants to try again, and meantime is working full-time with AIDS victims; a Dominican sister; an artist (no religion), who had been in squatters digs until Michael picked him up, brought him home, and got him into art college; a German friend of the artist, who has come to visit; an older woman named Doris, who goes home midweek; a priest from Hyth; a girl from an old Catholic family; a drunk that Michael brought in off the road, and after six months discovered was a priest; a lad from Northern Ireland who came for one night and stayed four years; a man just out of prison, who was released to Michael for a month; and another artist—a girl—who has set up her studio upstairs.

Londoner Margaret Ulloa spent a couple of wildly unforgettable years as a member of Hollings's impromptu community, which was then in the Southall parish house, where Michael was pastor (in fact, it was there Margaret met Luis, the priest from Ecuador whom she married).

"It's an extraordinary house to live in," Margaret says. "People come in and out of the house, youngsters wander in for a cup of coffee and to read the newspaper. There are people of all sorts coming in to see Michael all the time with their problems. People mistake Michael as some kind of wonder-worker. In fact, his greatest gift is in perceiving what people are capable of. He has a way of asking you to do things so that you have confidence you can do it."

But lest she give a false impression, Margaret says, "I assure you, life with Michael Hollings is no heavenly light. He'll have you working sixteen hours a day. But then he works twenty. If he realizes he's wasting your time or his, he'll cut. And he can be harsh and critical and crotchety, and needn't appear at all charismatic. And he can put you in your place if you need it."

There was that awful moment when Michael was addressing a group of very important nuns—it was at the annual taking of vows. "Sisters," said Michael in the homily, "remember always you are looking ahead to Jesus, not behind to Mother General."

Margaret says Michael Hollings seems to be living a totally fruitful life. "Everybody's last resort is always Michael, when things go wrong. But there has to be some untouched inner bit to make this possible," she believes. "A sort of hole in the middle. He does in fact do one hour of prayer, from five to six o'clock, every morning of his life. I know; I lived in the same house."

Michael Hollings is a big man, his hair still dark, with a habit of chuckling gently before he tells something that amuses him.

"There've been many times I've had total frustration with the Church, with individual bishops and clergy. But also with myself, y'see. Sometimes you wonder how you will survive without taking to the bottle.

"I was someone who wanted to go ahead and work on Vatican Two. I was in favor of birth control—that kind of background. Although, I'm a funny sort of a mix: I can see the value of the old as well as the new. I like the Tridentine Mass, for example.

"But I cannot see myself as having any power or effect outside the Church's ministry. I have no qualifications except the priesthood. I'd have to go for retraining. I suppose it comes down to celibacy: I always say I'd be an extremely poor husband—I'm so busy doing other things. My poor wife and children, they would fall by the wayside.

"Celibacy does give me freedom, but that's personal to me. Because there are married people who find more time to do things than I do. What I'd love to see is a situation where celibate priests and married priests could all be in the same racket together."

Michael Hollings is not sure if celibacy is a charism, that is, a special gift from God. He thinks in more down-to-earth terms. "In any work you find three kinds of people. I remember some people in Oxford, they wanted a degree, really, so they could get married and settle down. They weren't interested in a great career. That's the first kind of people."

The second type, Hollings says, are the people wholly dedicated to achievement: "the people determined to get to the top of Everest. Actors and so forth. They marry almost on the side. The first thing is their vision. Now to some extent, that is what happens with the priestly vocation.

"Then there is the third kind, the sort of universal aunt. Like women who never get married but look after everyone else. I don't see that any of them are charisms. They are just a natural development of men or women."

Michael Hollings sees himself as one of those universal aunts and thinks there is a place in the priesthood for all three types. But if there is, there is a place for marriage too.

What does Michael Hollings see as his greatest strength?

"That would be a rather proud thing to say, wouldn't it? It isn't easy to say—maybe that one has to take risks. I mean, I find myself getting hauled over the coals by bishops, more than most priests. Especially if I do something on the progressive side. As, when I do things like blessing a marriage for a divorced couple."

Is he not then putting his judgment before that of the Church?

"I don't think the Church is always right. I mean, she changes her stance many times. For example, in 1959 on a television program, I was asked why the mass was all in Latin. I said there's no reason why it couldn't be in English. That came out in the Catholic press, and I was summoned to Cardinal Godfrey. He said. 'Latin is the liturgical language, and you are never to say that again.' I was then summoned to the apostolic delegate, as I had been denounced to Rome. He said that in future I ought to write down anything I was going to say in public."

What about loneliness?

"I had had a girlfriend when I was in the army and she eventually married somebody else. What I found most difficult in the early days [of my priesthood] was when all my contemporaries were getting married—some of them were getting me to do their weddings. I felt tremendous loneliness going back at night."

"The loneliest was in the early years. After that I was fortunate to be out in a university situation. In the following ten or eleven years, I had youngsters in and out, morning, noon, and night, as chaplains do. There was just no time for loneliness. They were so friendly and loving.

"Then subsequently I developed my notorious 'open door' family. Since I started the open house in 1959, I've not nearly such problems with loneliness. And now that I'm so used to it, I'd find it very difficult to live in a shut-in presbytery with two priests or by myself."

* * *

It takes God a long time to fashion a mature and holy priest. For many it's a lifetime of struggle. Some leave and grow to maturity in marriage and parenthood, and some stay and do that same maturing in their priestly life of ministry (and some, of course, never mature at all, inside or outside the ministry).

There are distinctive marks about men who stay and remain genuinely celibate, and attain real maturity or are growing toward it. These marks are apparent in a man like Hollings, but the same qualities recur over and over in other such priests. To begin with, they all seem to know how to pray. And they do quite a lot of it. Too, most have a quite a sense of humor.

They appear as men who have taken responsibility for their lives. They are givers rather than receivers. An Irishman, Fr. Andy Horgan, once my pastor in Aberdeen, in the state of Washington, is now known as Seattle's "waterfront priest." He once recalled for the *Seattle Times* his first visit back to Ireland as a young returned missionary.[2] "There was a big crowd of relatives and friends out to greet me. We went to a pub and my brother bought the first round of drinks. When we downed that, my cousin bought a round. Then another cousin bought a round. Then my great-uncle, Connie Mahoney, looked at me squarely and growled, 'Andrew, stand your round.'

"I have never forgotten that," Andy says today. "Always stand your round. Don't be a leech, don't be a freeloader."

That's true of them all. These men aren't freeloaders: They give rather than take.

Most of them are not afraid to weep, or to be angry. And their features do not have that gray neutral mask that hides their real feelings.

They have tolerance and understanding toward men who leave, and they usually want what is good for them rather than what seems good for the institution. Usually they want such men back working with them and often go after them to invite them to do so.

Many want priests to be free to marry, even though they might not choose that option for themselves (a *New York Times*–CBS poll shows that of all U.S. priests, 55 percent would favor optional celibacy,[3] while a poll of bishops by Terrance Sweeney has 25 percent of those who responded in favor).[4]

Fr. Tim O'Connell, director of the Institute of Pastoral Studies in Chicago, notes four common elements in the life-style of most fulfilled and happy priests.[5] First, he believes, they truly enjoy the work of priestly ministry—which includes "caretaking," nurturing people in survival, growth, and development, as well as relating flexibly to many different kinds of people in many different ways as friend, confidant, teacher, leader, or mentor. "Men who don't like that work don't end up as happy priests," he says. "There is no substitute for this."

Second, he says, "I notice that these priests all have a private life that is clearly distinct from their professional, ministerial life. The job does not own them: They are not workaholics." In other words, they have achieved *individuation,* the establishment of an identity and life that is separate from their role.

Third, O'Connell is struck by the fact that these men have distanced themselves from the issues and agendas of the institutional Church: "These priests simply don't care about the internal politics of Church life, and if they ever had them, they have abandoned their ecclesiastical ambitions. They don't go out of their way to make trouble for the wider institution. But when it appears clear that the institution's agenda is something other than the good of the people, they opt for the people."

Lastly, he says, "The happy priests whom I know have all dealt with the issue of intimacy in their lives." Instead of moaning about celibacy or escaping into alcoholism, workaholism, abusive sex, or endless hobbies, these men have taken steps to meet the needs of intimacy. "In some cases they have done so through some sort of group life. There are members of religious communities who have made their community life an example of authentic and committed family life. There are diocesan priests who have formed prayer groups, support groups, deeply caring friendship groups. There are recovering alcoholics who experience a broad range of intimate sharing in their AA group.

"In other cases, these happy priests have developed individual relationships that meet their intimacy needs. The ways that these relationships define themselves, the specification of the partner (male/female, religious/lay, single/married), and the frequency of interaction vary widely. But the common denominators are that it is a genuinely reciprocal, self-revelatory relationship, not a disguised occasion for ministry, and that it is a close relationship that does, in fact, meet the intimacy needs of the priest."

*   *   *

People were shocked when a novel by Fr. Andrew Greeley described a celibate priest, Kevin Brennan, loving Ellen Foley chastely.[6] Yet deep friendships, sometimes love, between celibate priests and women have a long and honorable history. There was a celebrated thirteenth-century friendship between St. Dominic and Blessed Diana d'Andalo. According to the breviary, she became a nun, making her vows at the hands of St. Dominic, "whom she loved with all the ardour of her soul."[7] And St. Francis de Sales, the bishop of Geneva, had a famous relationship with St. Jane Françoise de Chantal.

One of the best-known friendships of all was that between Pope Pius XII and his housekeeper, a nun named Mother Pasqualina. He met her in the 1920s when she was a quite beautiful young German nun and he was a rising young monsignor in the Vatican diplomatic service. He asked her order if she could become his housekeeper, and she remained with him until he died. He turned to her for help and counsel in practically everything he did. When he became pope in 1939, she too moved into the Vatican, where she proceeded to rule the papal household with a rod of iron. They called her "the Popessa." The Curia detested her, and French Cardinal Tisserant ordered her out of the Vatican the very day the pope died.[8]

Psychologists tell us that most people are unable to mature without some kind of intimacy at some point in their lives, or at least a very deep relationship. It has its dangers, of course, but a life without love or a deep relationship, a life to which clerical training has condemned thousands of priests, is far more dangerous, far more stunting to growth. Love is less dangerous than no love at all.

The great French thinker, Fr. Teilhard de Chardin, loved three different women at different times in his life. While in Beijing, China, in the early 1930s he was deeply in love with an American woman, Lucille Swan. The intensity of his love drove him to ponder his celibacy more than he had ever done. A brief paper, "The Evolution of Chastity," records his thinking at the time.[9] In it he wonders why he does not make love to Lucille. Is it just that he is conditioned from childhood? Or by a desire to be faithful to a long history of moral duty and respectful admiration?

Teilhard always sees the material world as evolving toward something spiritual, and love is one of the greatest forces leading to

God. He sees two kinds of love, sexual love and love of God, and two possible ways they can be combined to lead to God.

The first is complete sexual union, with its enormous release of energies that can lead to God. The second way, Teilhard says, is that of the celibate: to keep only those elements of the mutual attraction that can lift up the partners in their mutual approach; to fly to each other in an upward movement; to love each other, and to deflect that love upward toward God. The spiritual power of the flesh remains, but it leaves room for virginity.

Teilhard says there are "two solutions. Two ways. On this point individual testimonies oppose and contradict each other. By birth, I can say, I find myself committed to the second way. I have followed it as far as possible. Of course, I have known difficult passages on this journey but I have never felt diminished in it, or lost."

The fact is that most men, celibate and noncelibate, will encounter romantic love at some point in their lives. The Jungian analyst Robert Johnson calls it the single most powerful experience most of us will have. And celibate priests are not immune.

CHAPTER 8

The Shadow Side of Celibacy

My gut tells me that all is not well, and that there is some kind of malaise among us clergy. No one is saying too much.

Fr. Ray Brady

FATHER Hans lives in a calendar picture. His little white church with its onion-domed tower nestles in the v of a hauntingly lovely German valley; timbered houses cluster around the church as if for protection; green pastures ascend the valley slopes on either side, to disappear intriguingly into the dark woods above.

One of the timbered houses is the rectory. It is a Sunday afternoon and I am sitting with Father Hans in the tidy livingroom as he tells me of the woman and child he keeps hidden in a city one hundred miles away. Father Hans is of medium height, gentle except for a powerful handshake, with a trimmed reddish beard and bright blue eyes. He is a young-looking forty-five.

"My son is eight years old," he tells me. "And he's getting restive. Gretchen is having a hard time with him just now. You see, he keeps asking where his father is, and she tells him his father is gone, she doesn't know where.

114

"He thinks I am his uncle. I drive to see them a couple of times a month. And sometimes I bring them down to stay here for a weekend, around Christmas or Easter. I tell people it's my sister-in-law and her kid. But it's getting harder and harder all the time."

So why not leave? I ask.

"It's the priesthood. It means so much to me. I cannot leave the priesthood, not for anything. Besides, what would I be fit for, now?"

The room has the bleak neatness that a man achieves without a woman. There is a kind of airless, bachelor smell. The armchairs are functional rather than elegant and seem little used. On the left wall is a crucifix made of two gnarled and twisted branches, on which an anguished Christ arcs His body and writhes. Beside it is a group photograph of Pope John Paul II with some men in black cassocks and purple sashes.

"It's getting harder and harder to keep this a secret," Hans says. "And it's getting to us both, more and more."

There is a long pause.

"And worse things have happened."

I notice his knuckles are white and tight, his fists pushed together in his lap.

"Last year she got pregnant again. But there was no way we could keep one more child a secret." His fists are grinding together. "So we decided on an abortion."

Hans opens his fists and puts his head in his hands. I look up at the gnarled Jesus, saying nothing. An alpine clock is tock-tock-tocking somewhere out in the hall. I want to say, "Is the priesthood worth this?," but I can't find the courage.

Father Hans looks up and his eyes are liquid. "Someday," he says, "I must stand before God and answer for what I have done. But those men"—he points to the picture—"will stand beside me. Their rules drove me to this."

Three days later I was visiting a woman named Anne Lueg in her home in Solingen, Germany, where she lives with her three children and her priest-husband, now a prominent figure in Germany's Christian Democratic party. Anne runs an organization to help women who are sexually involved with priests and has three hundred names on her books. I asked her how many children she personally knows who have been fathered by active priests.

"How about fifty?" she answered promptly.

And how many abortions? I asked.

"Ten that I know of, at this moment," she said.

Anne has already published a book, *Ein Sprung in der Kette* *("A Break in the Chain")*, in which the story of some of those fatherings are told,[1] and similar volumes have been published in both Germany and France, for instance, *Unheilige Ehen ("Unholy Wedlock")* by Ursula Goldman-Posch.[2]

Thousands of miles and three months later, I found myself at Canadensis, Pennsylvania, in a house deep in the woods from which Cathy Grenier runs a nonprofit organization called Good Tidings, which helps women who have become involved with priests. She has over seven hundred women on her books.

Cathy took over as director of Good Tidings from Maggie Olsen, who had founded the group after a women friend took her own life when dumped by a priest-lover. Cathy is a young woman with loving and caring enough to embrace all those seven hundred women and their men (who include three bishops). Her husband, Joe, a French Canadian and priest, backs her every step of the way. They keep open house for the women who need help, and these women frequently come to stay.

Upward of a hundred of the priests themselves have been in contact with her. Sometimes they too come to visit: It is sometimes the only place they can turn to. There is a rough-and-ready monthly retreat at the Greniers for any who want to come. Somehow there are camp beds or floors to lie on, and somehow there is food on the table.

Celibacy is not chastity. Celibacy is merely the permanent state of being unmarried. Chastity, for an unmarried person, means abstaining from genital sexual activity. And the tragedy begins when a priest is celibate but not chaste (which can easily happen when celibacy has not really been freely chosen by the priest).

Of great concern is what has happened to women, as this is so obviously celibacy's shadow side—the hidden cost of imposing it indiscriminately on every priest. It is the price paid, or exacted, by some priests who choose not to leave, yet do not, or cannot, observe celibacy's demands. Some priests? How many? How long a shadow does celibacy cast around the world?

Germany's Catholic News Agency (KNA) on January 30,

1985, released the findings of a questionnaire administered to the clergy in the Archdiocese of Cologne and answered by 27 percent of the priests. Question thirteen of the questionnaire asked if these men believed "a certain number of priests live celibacy only outwardly, and that, hidden from public view, they evade celibacy through numerous compromises." Seventy-four percent of the diocesan priests and 88 percent of the order priests answered yes.[3]

Stephan Pfürtner, writing in the Catholic journal *Concilium*, said, "It is no longer a secret that at least a part of the clergy can no longer—for a variety of reasons—accept compulsory celibacy. Have a few men, such as the Pope and bishops, really the right to dispose of the lives of thousands of other men, even against the convinced consciences of those men?"[4]

Fr. William Wells, an active priest now fourteen years ordained, writing in the Franciscan magazine, *St. Anthony Messenger*, says that "mandatory celibacy has become the millstone around the neck of the priesthood and is threatening to destroy it."[5] The law of celibacy, he notes, is routinely flouted by many priests, some of whom have secretly married and pass off their wives as live-in housekeepers in the rectory. Others, he says, have taken lovers. The law, he continues, has also led to "rampant psychosexual problems," including a huge increase in reported cases of child molesting and a "noticeable increase in the number of gay seminarians" at Catholic divinity schools.

A committee of bishops has been established by America's National Conference of Catholic Bishops to examine the problem of sexual abuse by priests.[6]

An editorial in Britain's *Catholic Herald* on May 8, 1987, said, "What is clear is that a blind eye is being turned to the large, indeed increasing amount, of unhappy priests and the very high incidents of homosexuality and drunkenness among clergy, due, ultimately, to loneliness."[7]

In Holland, Father Pieter cycles home each evening from his pastoral assignment in the Diocese of Rotterdam. He wheels his bicycle up the pathway to the two front doors of the semidetached house where he lives. The doors are side by side, and his name is on the left-hand one. One the right-hand door his neighbor's name is clearly written: Jolanda van Rijn.

Father Pieter put his key in the left-hand door and lets himself in. Inside, the walls are down and it is one house. Jolanda is already home: He kisses her on both cheeks and they start preparing supper together.

One of Holland's most distinguished priests, a household name in his own country and a familiar name abroad, Father Jan has given a great deal of himself to the Church and to other people. He has also had a relationship with a woman for nearly fifteen years. The relationship of Father Jan and Karin is fairly well known, but not spoken about. "People tend to ignore things that they cannot put into categories," Jan says. "They can understand clear, fixed social forms like monastery or marriage." Anything else they sort of look past, without seeing or wanting to see.

I listened as Jan and a priest-colleague discussed how many other priests had relationships with women. They agreed on between 10 and 20 percent—"but that's just guessing," said the colleague.

One of the most famous "secret" relationships in Holland is that of Fr. Willem Berger and Henriëtte Röttgering. A priest of the Diocese of Haarlem and until he retired a couple of years ago, professor of the psychology of religion at Nijmegen University, Fr. Willem for the past twenty-five years has lived in an intimate relationship with Henriëtte. She was presented to the world as his housekeeper and secretary. If the relationship was secret, it was an open sort of secret. "It had been known to all the leading priests and people of my diocese," he tells me. "There was a kind of silent agreement—we know, but without speaking about it. A lot of the priests came to our home for meals." And for years he had been a consultant to his diocese.

In 1981, Willem and Henriëtte went public about their relationship. In an interview with *De Tijd* magazine, they told their story from start to finish. "I'm sticking my neck out," Berger told the magazine.[8]

Why did they choose to go public after all those years? Berger tells me it was the 1980 Special Synod of Dutch bishops that changed his mind. The bishops had come back from three weeks with the pope and had announced that, since the reasons for compulsory celibacy were self-evident, there was no need for further discussion. Celibacy was the only possible life-style for priests, they had said.

"To me, the Dutch bishops were breaking a solemn promise,"

Berger says. Ten years before, they had undertaken to continue to press the Dutch case for optional celibacy, so Berger now decided to speak out in the most effective way he knew.

I heard in Holland that it was Henriëtte that finally pushed him to go public. In an interview at the time, she said she had suffered terribly from the secrecy. "If you love each other, you want to share it with everybody," she said. She described those early years together as "a black time, of which I prefer not to think again. It's past."

Willem and Henriëtte are now married.

More than anyone, it is the women who get hurt. But a priest too can suffer terribly from remorse. Take, for example, this letter from a dying French priest to his bishop:

> Forgive my miserable cowardice in writing to you anonymously, but to do so otherwise would cost me enormous effort. . . .
>
> I am now a 72-year-old priest, seriously ill and condemned to die with a cancer—one or two months to live, they tell me. So I *must* write this letter to tell you the truth. . . .
>
> Father, I am a wretched man: 20 years ago, in the name of my vocation and in accordance with our consecrated way of life, I abandoned a woman in a cowardly fashion. Despite great difficulties in her life, she found a way to help me. . . . My priestly pride, my cowardice before the rule of the Church, meant that I broke everything off, not wanting even to offer her a word or a sign of friendship.
>
> Today, lucid and imagining what suffering my action must have caused her, I regard myself as the most unworthy of priests. Furthermore, I have never been able to retract this cowardice because the person concerned died four years afterwards. Since then I have been a bad priest, torn between the words which I preach and my own conduct. . . .
>
> Father, in the name of obedience and the rule of celibacy, I am dying with the greatest distrust for myself and for my priestly life. I haven't borne loyal and faithful

witness for Christ Jesus, from the very moment when I behaved in such a cowardly manner towards another human being who trusted me.

Father, pray for me. Help those others who are in the same position as me to have the courage to be honest men—the only way to find the Lord and peace for the soul, while waiting for the Church to revise her position on imposed celibacy.

This letter will make amends. A very tiny reparation at the end of a life, and a duty which I owe to this person's family and her son, who have, in spite of everything, maintained a charitable contact with me.[9]

Missionaries in Peru estimate that 80 percent of local priests live with women. But, one says, there is no way it could be otherwise. "The whole Andean culture is built around the concept of the *pareja* ('the couple'). Everything goes in couples—animals, the sun and the moon. There are even two mountains, male and female. The word for a single guy is *mula* ('mule').

"And up in the mountains, authority depends on having a family. You can't be celibate and be a community leader; you can't be established if you don't have a wife and children. The culture does not respect celibacy because a man is expected to shoulder responsibility, and that means the responsibility of a family."

In Brazil a group of native priests estimate that between 60 and 70 percent of native Brazilian priests have some sort of liaisons with women. A great many of those would be permanent relationships. A missionary says he believes one in three missionaries have their women.

A journalist, Tim Unsworth, who writes in the *National Catholic Reporter*, tells me that Cardinal Sin in the Philippines is closing his eyes to 50 percent of his priests living with women. I met with a group of Filipino priests who thought it a conservative estimate.

"In my deanery," one of them told me, "practically every priest is involved deeply with women." He explained that rural priests' houses are always full of relatives and extended family. "When I was newly ordained, I always took for granted that the kids playing around the rectory were the priest's nieces and nephews. It was only later I realized they were his children. They are not introduced as the priest's children, and the wife is never affirmed.

She is introduced as an aunt or a sister. It's a pitiful situation for her and the children.

"The parish sends the children to the local school and supports them. The people are hesitant to give to the collection because they know it's going to support the children. That's why collections in the Philippines are so small."

One Filipino priest told me he asked his bishop why he tolerated what he knew was going on.

"What else can I do?" the bishop replied. "I need these priests. They are all I have."

A missionary, returned from working in Zaire, Africa, tells me that all local priests in the diocese where he worked have fathered children. All have their women. "I would not say a woman, but women," the missionary says. "In African culture, if you are somebody you have two wives. Sometimes four or five wives. Now a priest is a man of honor: If he has two or more wives, no problem whatsoever. But the problem is the priest cannot marry officially. The women usually stay on the mission, have little huts near the mission. Everyone knows it—the bishop, the chief—it's common knowledge."

Some of the missionaries also have their women, this priest tells me. There was one Dutch priest who returned home to Holland, leaving behind a native woman and their child. One winter's day, some years later, she arrived unannounced at the Brussels airport in Belgium with her eight-year-old son. This simple African woman, who had never been outside her village, must have been of sterling character. She had collected money from all her relatives to enable her to go and seek out her man. She had negotiated the various airports and airlines to reach Belgium and had managed to contact him in Holland when she arrived.

He found mother and son shaking with cold in their wispy cotton clothes and sent them right back where they came from.

He continues to minister as a priest in Holland.

Luis Kaserer, a native of Bolsano in Italy, was a Mill Hill missionary priest working in Zaire in 1982. Then came Brigitte, a Dutch nurse, who was also sent to live and work at the mission station. "I was very much afraid," Luis tells me now. "How were we going to survive in the middle of the forest, me with a person as beautiful as that?"

They were left alone together on that mission for one and a half years. "Yet I must say, when we found a baby was on the way, it was a big shock," Luis says.

The couple went to break the news to the bishop, and to ask if they could stay on at the mission. The bishop said that Brigitte would have to go. Tell the mission her parents in Holland are seriously ill and she has to return home, he suggested. "Don't let yourself be troubled by a girl like that" was his private counsel to Luis.

A few days later the couple got back to the mission. "All the villages had heard Brigitte was pregnant," Luis says. "They had prepared a big reception for us. Everybody had come from miles around: There were lots of gifts and congratulations for Brigitte and myself."

Then the elders of the village took Luis aside to inform him of his change of status due to fatherhood. "You are no child [*mwana*] anymore. You are *ngolo* now," they told him. That meant he was now a real adult, a person of weight in the village. If a *ngolo* talks, people are supposed to listen.

The villagers then held a meeting of the parish council, which wrote a letter to the bishop, asking him not to send the couple away, as they were doing so much good in the district. "To have a child in Africa is the most essential thing," the letter said.

But Luis and Brigitte were sent away. They are now married in Holland.

A couple of years later Luis's identical twin, Konrad, also a Mill Hill missionary in Zaire, met and left to marry an American girl who had come to work on the mission.

We are told that the Church in Poland is flourishing, and it is a fact that one in three priests ordained in Europe is Polish. About this flourishing Church a young Polish woman spoke to a meeting of the Advent group in London. I quote from the group's bulletin. "She recounted that her experience, back home, was that any priest who decided that he would marry the woman he loved, was banished, along with his loved one. But—if he said nothing, life went along as before, and his children went to school with all the other villagers' children. Everybody just accepted the situation. With Vatican 'intelligence' superior to even the CIA, no one can say that John Paul II is unaware. *Qui tacet, consentit* ['Silence is consent']. Or, how double can your standards get?"[10]

A young Polish priest who ministers in a city diocese in Poland explained to me why he and some colleagues have no problem with breaking the rule of celibacy. "Compulsory celibacy is just a human law," he said. "Everyone knows it's going to change eventually. So why should our lives be spoiled by something that's going to change in twenty years' time? Also, in our case here in Poland, the [civil] law is corrupt since the first day we are born. Equality, for example, it's only on paper. What you can do, what you can get away with, that's the main thing. Celibacy is no different."

But, I asked, could not a woman get hurt when a priest behaves like that?

"The woman knows what she is getting into. Just like a woman who gets involved with a married man. She knows we cannot leave to marry, and she goes into it with her eyes open. So she deserves what she gets.

"For us, it's far more seriously wrong to leave and marry, than to have your woman. That's something that has come down to us from the partisans during the war. When people's lives depended on you as a partisan, it was treason to leave just to marry a woman. But to have a woman on the side, when you're a partisan, no trouble. It's the same for a priest today. We're still fighting a war."

In talking with active serving priests in many parts of the world, I have found there are five levels of relationships priests have with women.

First, there are priests who have a deep and lasting friendship with women, but without genital sex. This is the relationship described in Chapter 7, and such friendships can bring immense consolation and maturing to the individual priest, and benefit to the Church.

The second level of involvement is like the previous one, but with occasional physical sex. Even in totally celibate friendships, sexual attraction is a normal and healthy development, even when not physically acted out. But even the best people are human, and sometimes things happen.

Third, there are priests who have a permanent sexual relationship with one woman—a lover, a mistress, a common-law wife. Sometimes it's hidden for years. Sometimes the whole world, even the bishop, knows but chooses not to notice.

Fourth, there are priests who from time to time have sexual friendships with different women. These liaisons can occur consecutively or concurrently.

Lastly, there are priests who use their Roman collars as tomcats use their meows, to charm all the women they can and lure them to bed—and use their collars a second time around, to break the relationship or evade their responsibilities ("I'm a priest and I've got to end this," or, "I'm a priest, so you'll have to look after that child on your own"). These are the Elmer Gantrys of the Roman Catholic Church.

A prolonged encounter with priests in this last category is described here by a young married woman somewhere in the United States. She had been in an unhappy marriage for some years with two children and an unfaithful husband. The local pastor, whom she calls Father X, gave her a job as housekeeper and became her lover. "Father X took good care of me. Besides my salary as housekeeper, I received quite a bit of extra money from the church collection. He took many small bills from the Sunday evening mass collection when the money counters were not around. He bought me clothes, took me to nice restaurants, anticipated needs that I had forgotten I had. On days off we went camping or, if the weather was bad, went to motels.

"When Father X was away I was the pastor. I gave out the information for the bulletins, wrote the parish letters, stole the $1 bills from the 6:30 collection, opened and took care of his mail, etc.

"In our parish there was an assistant pastor . . . Father Y. He always made passes at me but I never returned the favor. One time when Father X was in another state, Father Y had just been dumped by a true love. He was extremely depressed. I tried to cheer him up by cooking for him, reading to him, playing cards . . . whatever. One day we were playing gin and he made the bet that if he won he would rape me and if I won I would rape him. I thought that was real funny. He won. He raped me.

"When Father X came back I told him about it. He got on the phone to the personnel board to have Father Y removed. I heard him say, 'Get rid of Jacko—he's up to his old tricks again.'

"It wound up we all stayed. I made love to both of them (at different times). I separated from my husband. He took my older child and I stayed in our home with the baby. Somehow, the two priests became friends. X didn't know I was 'seeing' Y; Y knew I was seeing X, but didn't care. We became a threesome.

"There were parties. All the priests of the inner sanctum would have parties at least once a month—sometimes in the rectories—

sometimes in their mistresses' houses. I noticed that there were different types of relationships. Some were truly married in spirit and would never think of being unfaithful. Most were stringing along many women.

"It was an exciting time for me . . . and it was a lie. I discovered that Father X was seeing other women when he was making hospital visits or playing golf. I called the other women. It was ugly. Some very hurtful things happened.

"Father X came out of the whole mess unscathed. I came out with nothing—no parish, no reputation, no money, no love.

"I accept responsibility for my involvement with these two priests. I needed love and took it from the wrong people."[11]

Statistics are understandably hard to come by, but there are some. Richard Sipe is a married priest who holds a teaching appointment as lecturer in psychiatry in the department of psychiatry at Johns Hopkins Medical School. He has just concluded a twenty-five-year study of U.S. priests, using fifteen hundred informants, of the practice, process, and achievement of clerical celibacy.[12] Celibacy, for the purpose of the study, is defined as "a freely chosen state, usually vowed, that involves an honest and sustained attempt to live without direct sexual gratification in order to serve others productively for a spiritual motive (in response to grace)." Sipe obviously takes celibacy as meaning not just being unmarried, but being chaste as well. However, he believes his definition allows for human frailty, without compromising essential integrity by denial or rationalization.

In an address delivered in Washington, D.C. on June 17, 1988, Sipe summarized the results of the study. "I estimate that at any one time no more than 50 percent of American priests practice celibacy. No more than 2 percent of clergy have, with certainty, achieved celibacy without any major impediment, with an additional 3 to 6 percent relatively well enough established in celibate practice to say they have achieved it.

"These figures are not an indictment of good men struggling to reach an ideal. Nor are they a critique of that minority who may not give a damn and use their priesthood as a cover for sexual indulgence. What they form, rather, is a serious invitation to the Church to face important questions. What is celibacy? How is it practiced? What is the process? How does one achieve sexual identity without sexual experiences? How does one remain celibate after sexual experience? How is celibacy achieved?"[13]

Sipe's study also indicates that about 20 percent of priests have ongoing sexual liaisons ("this is low," Sipe says, "compared to some other cultures where the estimates run above 50 percent"). Another 8 to 10 percent have occasional affairs.

If Sipe's figures were to be matched on a worldwide basis, we would be talking of well over two hundred thousand priests failing to observe celibacy, to add to the one hundred thousand who have already left and married.

Up until recently, Sipe says, fewer than 20 percent of clergy were of homosexual orientation or undetermined in orientation, of which one fourth, or 5 percent of total clergy, had a regular homosexual partner and another 7 percent had periodic sexual acting out with a number of partners. However, Sipe notes, reports of homosexual activity have increased significantly since 1978, in some areas closer to 40 percent, if one isolates the figures from 1978 to 1985.

This growth in both homosexual orientation and activity, particularly in certain seminaries and among some newer priests, I have found to be a talking point among clergy throughout the world. Two different bishops acknowledged to me their awareness of and concern about it—one of them being Dom Helder Camara. No one quite understands the reasons for this trend, but it cannot be too glibly blamed on compulsory celibacy, since some Protestant denominations, even with married clergy, are encountering the same phenomenon.

But there are connections. As Richard P. McBrien puts it in an article in *Commonweal:* "It is not inconceivable that the ordained priesthood is attractive to certain people precisely because it excludes marriage. To put it plainly: as long as the Church requires celibacy for the ordained priesthood, the priesthood will always pose a particular attraction for gay men who are otherwise not drawn to ministry," because, he says, it gives them "occupational respectability and freedom from social suspicion."[14]

Compulsory celibacy does not work. And it is being rejected by priests all around the world. Silence has been imposed by Rome, but these men are voting with their feet.

Heinz-Jürgen Vogels has written a treatise on compulsory celibacy entitled *The Devil's Sieve.*[15] It's an apt title. And it is a sieve through which relatively few pass.

"By their fruits you shall know them," Jesus said, and the

fruits of compulsory celibacy are those thousands of men leading double lives, thousands of women leading destroyed lives, thousands of children spurned by their ordained fathers, to say nothing of the priestly walking wounded, the psychiatric cases, the alcoholics and the workaholics, the gray lonely faces that witness to the wretched lives of so many priests of Jesus Christ. Only Satan could invent such a sieve for the priesthood.

The good and wonderful men, described in Chapter 7, who have achieved true celibacy in their lives, are no justification of compulsory celibacy. They do not even need it: Their celibacy is a free choice, and such men, and women too, will always be with us.

To see compulsory celibacy as justified by its relatively sparse successes is to make the same mistake that Haig, Joffre, Ludendorf, and all the rest of the generals made in World War I. From the trenches they cheerfully sent hundreds of thousands of men over the top to their deaths, so that a few survivors could succeed in taking the enemy placement. They had no problems with the massive casualty rate. Their proportions were wrong, their hearts were hard, and history had branded them as brutal buffoons. And so will history—and God—judge us, the Church, and our general staff in the Vatican, if we indulge in the same kind of thinking.

But do our men in the Vatican know?

A document prepared for the bishops at the Vatican Council by one of the council's experts (or *periti*, as they were called), which has come into my possession, told the council fathers of the massive abandonment of celibacy throughout the world, and that was over a quarter of a century ago. The document, still stamped "Sub Secreto," uses some graphic images: "Rightly or wrongly a good number of priests who are in the ministry are not free from accusations of immorality, have conducted themselves so notoriously that it is a torture and a trial to be a priest in some parts of the world. In the cases of at least some priests in all dioceses, not allowing them to marry is like not allowing them to go for their essential needs. They stifle the whole atmosphere with bad and suffocating odour. 'Celibacy is like Prohibition in India,' said once an elderly priest to the writer. This may be an overstatement and yet how many can throw the first stone?"[16]

These words were written for the bishops of the Vatican Council, and read by them. And then stamped "secret" and quietly filed away.

Yes, our men in the Vatican know. And not from that document alone: Their information service would be a respectable rival to the CIA. They could write this chapter for me. Yet they are silent, and they seem to be very frightened.

It is not so certain how much is known to bishops around the world today. I shared Sipe's figures with Cardinal Hume when we met in November 1988, and it was clear to me that he was deeply shocked and distressed. I mentioned at the time that I was worried whether I should even publish these figures for fear of the scandal they might give. He thought for a few moments and then said quietly, "Be objective. That's really all you can do."

If bishops do not know, it is because no one is talking enough. "Celibacy has become a lot like cancer," say a U.S. bishop quoted by the *Chicago Tribune*. "Too many bishops just don't want to talk about it, and hope that the problems associated with it will simply go away. But the conspiracy of silence is doing all of us more harm than good."

According to Catholic psychologists I have worked with for this book, the silence of the Roman Catholic Church can be understood in terms of the two concepts of *denial* and *secrets*.

Denial is one of the classic ways of dealing with unacceptable reality. Refusing to recognize the "shadow side" of celibacy is tantamount to such denial, which can occur not only in individuals but in organizations. The collective denial, by ourselves and our Church hierarchy, of the reality of celibacy's shadow side is quite simply an immature response. The wretchedness and misery it brings down on the Church cannot be faced or cured as long as this denial continues.

The other way to understand Church silence is in terms of family secrets, as outlined in Napier and Whitaker's classic treatise, *The Family Crucible*.[17] There are certain kinds of family secrets that are bad for the family. Some secrets reflect a whole family in trouble, and those problems cannot be dealt with if kept under wraps and never discussed—problems like a parent's alcoholism, sexual abuse of the children, an extramarital affair, homosexuality in a parent or child. It is like having an elephant in the family room, with everyone walking around it and no one saying the elephant is there. There is the fantasy that if the secret or embarrassment is not discussed, it will go away. Instead, it makes things worse.

We have maintained secrets for many years about popes, bishops, and priests, and we hold on to those secrets until forced to deal with them by public outcry. But secrets in this great family that is the Church, the family bonded by Christ, are particularly destructive. They interfere with family communication, withhold essential information, and deny problems. The problems never get resolved, and the seeds of Church pathology, disturbance, and discontent grow.

It was Carl Rogers, one of America's most respected psychologists, who said that to solve a problem one has first to own that problem and take responsibility for it.

It was Jesus who said, "Woe to you Pharisees, who bind burdens on men's backs and will not stir a finger to lighten them."

It was Pope John XXIII who said in 1963, shortly before his death, in a conversation with his old friend Etienne Gilson:

"Do you want me to tell you what is my greatest worry? I do not mean as a human being, but as a pope, I am continually vexed by the thought of those young priests who so courageously carry the burden of ecclesiastical celibacy. For some among them it is a martyrdom. Yes, a kind of martyrdom. It often seems to me that I hear a sort of complaint—from here, but from much farther—as if voices were asking the Church to take that burden away from them."[18]

CHAPTER 9

In Search of a
Root Cause

*A Church that bears the name of Jesus, heeds his
word, and is impelled by his Spirit, must never be
identified with a particular class, caste, clique or bureaucracy.*

Hans Küng

WHEN Columbus sailed for America, the Black Abbey in Kilkenny,
Ireland, was already over 250 years old. Today, after almost eight
centuries of existence, it still functions as a church. There is now a
tiny oratory built on to it, which has a window looking down over
the altar. This is where the priests of the church can come to pray.

During the late 1960s I knelt at that window, hour after hour,
day after day, looking down at the tabernacle and praying for deliverance. Deliverance from what, I did not know. Often the only
prayer I could think of was the one from the Garden—"Let this
chalice pass from me," which I would literally say over and over.
Nor, in my aloneness, did I know what I know now—that while I
knelt there, thousands of other priests were kneeling in anguish in
every corner of the world, most believing themselves totally alone
in their unthinkable thoughts and also praying for deliverance.

I have met hundreds of these men, and heard the stories of why they left. Some sought deliverance for smothering authority; some could no longer preach certain things they did not hold; some left to marry.

Can these be reduced to one underlying reason whereby so many thousands left in such a brief span of time, and are still leaving? Is there a root cause?

Terry Dosh believes it is the mid-twentieth-century discovery of freedom, the need for liberation. But from what are they seeking liberation?

Is it from a celibate life? Certainly the desire to marry permeates many a decision to leave, and a loving relationship with a woman often seems to tip the scales. But there are indications of more underlying reasons.

An investigation by Fr. Andrew Greeley and Richard Schoenherr, published by the U.S. bishops in 1972, found the most frequently mentioned very important reason for priests' leaving was "a feeling that they could no longer live within the structure of the Church."[1]

The English Dominican, Fr. Conrad Pepler, champion and friend to many priests who leave, would substantially agree with Greeley and Schoenherr but appends an insight on why it is happening at this particular point: "The fact that all these men are quite suddenly asking for dispensation must have a root cause, and, as far as I can see, that cause is, indirectly, Vatican II. The Council had raised hopes for a new, or at least a renewed, dynamism in mission and ministry. But they did not see much change in the general structure of the Church, so that instead of a new drive, an uncertainty about the nature and mission of the priesthood developed. The possibility of dispensation from the commitment to priestly vocation, hitherto practically unknown, seemed to offer an escape from these painful uncertainties."[2]

In sum, priests leave because they perceive the changes in thinking at Vatican II have not been made concrete through parallel changes in structures. I would take this one step further and suggest that the particular structure that irks most, and the structure that drives these priests out, is something called *clericalism*. It is a hypothesis that would need testing, but it seems to me, nearly two decades after Greeley's report, that almost all the reasons people give for leaving can be reduced ultimately to clericalism. And it explains why so many of these men insist they have not left the Church, or the priesthood, or even the ministry. The only other thing they could have left is the clerical condition.

What is this clericalism, and is it separable from priesthood? Fr. Yves Congar describes it as a caricature of what priesthood should be.[3] The late Fr. Thomas Merton called it a *caste:* "The discipline of the medieval church required a celibate, clerical caste," he wrote. "It can be argued that in the modern world such a caste is a liability. . . ."[4]

Clericalism is an elusive concept, hard to define, and it's easier to describe a lot of things about clericalism than to say what it is. Let me sketch a picture or two.

Once in the 1960s, when I was a priest in Kilkenny, Ireland, I returned late from Dublin. It was a long drive, and I had not eaten, so I went down to a stall in a nearby alleyway to buy fish and chips. The pubs had just closed, and there was a line of about twenty people waiting at the little mobile stall. The streetlights in the alley had gone out and it was quite dark. I got into conversation with the man in line ahead of me. We exchanged the usual remarks on the weather, he told me a simple joke he had just heard in the pub, and I told him one in return. Just two men passing a few minutes in a friendly way.

As the line moved forward, the light from the stall suddenly fell on my Roman collar. "O God," said the man, "I didn't know you were a priest, Father. I never knew priests liked chips, Father." There was a long and painful pause. Then he continued, "Father, I hope I didn't say anything that, uh—well, I didn't know you were a priest, y'see, Father. Sorry about them jokes, Father."

I tried to revive the conversation, but the rapport was shattered; the man was so embarrassed he could not look me in the eye. My collar had fulfilled its function superbly: Once again it had cut me off from an ordinary human being.

That is the essence of clericalism: It is a kind of ecclesiastical apartness, whereby priests are cut off from the rest of people. Whereas Jesus walked the roads among people, ate in their houses, sat by a well talking to a woman, the clerics are deliberately cut off from people and formed into a special caste.

The cutting off is accomplished in a number of different ways. The most obvious is by dress. The wearing of black suits, of skirtlike cassocks, of the powerfully symbolic collar, cuts the priest off in several distinguishing ways.

First, it sets very distinct limits on his behavior. Second, it controls how people perceive him and thus controls their behavior toward him. That powerful symbol, the necktie, says much to people. So does wearing skirts (remember the term ''unfrocked''?). I remember hearing that in Ireland, when men's trousers first had buttoned flies, this was not true of priests' trousers, which had no flies for many years after that. That must indeed have created certain ambivalent perceptions about the priests.

But more than anything else, his dress controls how the priest perceives the world around him. People's behavior changes the instant they perceive a cleric in their midst—which means that he can never see people as they really are, except if he happens to line up for fish and chips in a dark alleyway.

Let there be no doubt that this condition was intended for all clerics and religious—priests, brothers, nuns. The Christian Brothers' rule prohibited them ''from frequent and unnecessary conversations with seculars,'' and ''from engaging in political conversations with assistant [lay] teachers.'' The Sisters of Mercy required their members to avoid ''unnecessary secular intercourse,'' and the Presentation Sisters had this rule: ''When spoken to by men, of any state or profession, they shall observe and maintain the most guarded reserve, never fix their eyes on them, nor show themselves, in conversation or otherwise, in the least degree familiar with them, how devout or religious soever they may be.''[5]

The seminary was the great breeder of clerical apartness. In the wake of the Reformation, the sixteenth-century Council of Trent set out to make the priest a creature apart, and education was the means. The child was to be got before the world had tainted him, and he was to be raised totally apart.

In many parts of the world, boys as young as eleven, sometimes even nine, were taken into the seminary, dressed in little cassocks, and reared apart from the world. ''Cradle snatching'' was the contemptuous term we Irish priests reserved for it—hardly realizing that entering seminary at sixteen or seventeen, as we had done, was little better.

Cradle snatching is not ended: Don Razotti, rector of the seminary in Reggio Emilia, Italy, told me in 1987 that they still accept eleven-year-olds: ''They end up clearer about what a vo-

cation is, and clearer about the function of a priest,'' he explained
to me.

Seminary education results in a phenomenon called foreclo-
sure, whereby the life choices open to the young person are closed
too soon. Psychologists believe that this can halt personal development, both emotional and intellectual, resulting in a too-close iden-
tification of the person with his clerical profession. ''The seminary
aim,'' says psychologist Don Conroy, ''is to draw the person and
his role so close that they cannot be separated. That's damaging.''
I have chronicled in earlier chapters the consequent agonies after a
man leaves the clerical state and attempts to separate person and role
for the first time.

Military academies throughout the world have used seminary
techniques (isolation from outside, fostering an elite mentality) to
create officer castes.[6] But even officers can marry, and none of these
castes depends on the quite incredible isolating factor of compulsory
celibacy. That, more than anything else, is what sets the clerical
caste apart. As Richard Sipe says, ''There is no other class . . .
where part of their identity is defined by the sacrifice of their
sexuality.''[7]

What then is the clerical caste, and why has it come to be? A
corps of professional ministers is of course necessary. ''Beliefs
evoke structure,'' as sociologist Max Weber pointed out.[8] All reli-
gions evolve some kind of administrative structure: a group of se-
lected people who are the guardians of the sacred event (which for
Christians is the Resurrection), and who have the authority to teach
and defend it. Without them, there would be a chaos in beliefs.[9]

Robert K. Merton, another sociologist, has shown that professional groups, and especially bureaucracies, easily degenerate. They
end up defending their entrenched interests, putting their own existence, and above all, the extension of their own power, before the
needs of those they were founded to serve.[10]

I believe clericalism is such a degeneration. It is that part of our
Church, of ourselves, that has turned away from serving God's
people, from helping them reach God, and has set up the golden calf
of power and control over others, before which it now bows down
and worships.

Priests who leave are renouncing precisely that. And the men
who stay, those who grow into mature and holy priests, spurn it with

equal vehemence. When people perceive that the structures are impeding, instead of helping them reach God, then some sort of shattering of the structures occurs. It happened to the Anglicans a couple of centuries ago when John Wesley turned away from structures perceived as holding people back from God.

Clericalism is, first and last, separation for the sake of control. The Turks once had their Janissaries, Christian children taken by force, brought up in special seminaries to be fanatical celibate warriors for the Koran, never permitted to marry, totally controllable, going forth "to slay the enemies of the Sultan and of Allah with the inflamed and contracted fanaticism of a monk," as H.A.L. Fisher describes it.[11] The Zulu King Chaka had a corps of celibate warriors, equally controllable and formidable. It works. And clericalism, likewise, has delivered total control, from the top to the bottom of the Roman Catholic Church.

First, there has been control over the laity, by an elite corps of clerics whose separation both placed them on a pedestal and swathed their humanity in secrecy and mystery, and who could exact conformity by the fear of social disapproval, but even more by the fear of hell, diligently fostered in long-remembered sermons, retreats, and parish missions.

Far more important, though, within that corps there has been immense control by the higher clerics over the lower clerics. The means of that control include fear, rewards, a tradition of unquestioning obedience, and, above all, celibacy. The promise of obedience to the bishop made at ordination, combined with the belief that the superior's will was invariably the voice of God, left little room for individual conscience. The fears ranged from fear of hell for disobedience, to fear of unacceptable assignments and denied promotions, to fear of destitution and of becoming a pariah if one left the ministry. An honor system, with titles like "Canon" and "Monsignor," and a promotion system with ladders reaching to the highest level of hierarchy, took care of rewards. It had little to do with Christ's counsel about seeking the lowest place at the table, but it had a great deal to do with control.

Celibacy, of course, has been the control factor par excellence. Bachelors are quite simply easier to manage. There is no family to care for or pay for; there is no wife to counsel disobedience or to stiffen resolve; there is no danger of nepotism or of children inheriting church property—a very real problem for the Irish Church during the centuries after St. Patrick. "Clerical celibacy," says John P. Dolan, in his *History of the Reformation,* "was in many respects the final phase in the molding of a sacerdotal caste system, that came to identify the church with the clergy rather than with the entire body of believers. It formed an inseparable barrier between the layman and the clergy."[12]

It is little wonder that a famous book on management reckoned the Roman Catholic Church as one of the three most efficient organizations in history—the other two being General Motors and the nineteenth-century Prussian Army. But at a very high price: at the bottom, a clergy submissive and fearful and solitary; at the top, a hierarchy and curia answerable to no one.

There is a scene in *Barchester Towers,* Trollope's satire on nineteenth-century Anglican clericalism, in which the simple and godly old pastor asks Archdeacon Grantly what Jesus might say about certain local ecclesiastical shenanigans.

"This has nothing to do with Jesus Christ!" snaps the archdeacon.

Right he is. And neither has clericalism anything to do with Jesus Christ, although it has a lot to do with the Pharisees he denounced for seeking to lord it over people instead of serving them.

Christ provides the ultimate test—"By their fruits ye shall know them." What are the fruits of clericalism? While assessing them, let us remember that clericalism is not the Church, but rather something that is trying to hijack the Church.

First, the clerical institution puts its own survival first, and the needs of the people of God second. For just one example: because of a shortage of priests, thousands upon thousands of parishes around the world do not have the mass, the center point of the faith. If priests could marry, sociologists estimate that vocations alone would quadruple. But faced with a choice between the Eucharist for which people are crying out, and obligatory celibacy which might shore up clericalism, the clerical institution opts for celibacy and will not even permit discussion on it. Bare altars, priestless communities, and hungry sheep are thus among the fruits of clericalism.

Clericalism leads to a suppression of truth and of the freedom to think and communicate, which in the end drives out many priests.

Galileo was only the most famous case of such suppression: Today we have Hans Küng, Leonardo Boff, and Charles Curran. The late Karl Rahner, accepted now as one of the century's greatest theologians, was ordered to submit his every word for scrutiny by the clerics of the Vatican—"these ghastly bonzes," as he called them.[13]

Only a couple of years ago, the Jesuit Terrance Sweeney wrote to all the U.S. bishops to ask their views on optional celibacy. One quarter of those who replied were favorable, but Sweeney was ordered by the clerics of Rome to drop his research and suppress his findings.[14] He resigned rather than do that. In Brazil, Eduardo Hoornaert has been compiling a summa of liberation theology: Rome has attempted to suppress it.[15]

Clericalism breeds a paranoidal secrecy, which many priests say has driven them out of the clerical corps. Just as civil regimes use official secrets acts to cover up ineptitude or wrongdoing, citing state security, the clerical institution cites the danger of scandal and shrouds its every deed and misdeed in the deepest silence.

After the 1987 synod, a Canadian archbishop, Donat Chiasson, spoke of "Vatican civil servants obsessed with secrecy. What do we have to hide from people with whom we feel communion?" he asked, adding that he felt deceived by a system that makes real dialogue impossible.[16]

There is overpowering legalism. The clerics have replaced the Bible with the Code of Canon Law. Legalism is the sin of the Pharisees—putting mechanical obedience to regulations above the human needs of people, whom those rules were meant to serve. Many a dedicated priest has been turned off by such legalism and the little games of the Church lawyers. It was legalism that led the archbishop of Lund in 1213 to ask Pope Innocent III whether a man who had two concubines was ineligible to be ordained priest.[17] He was told that concubinage did not stand in the way of ordination.

It is a comparable legalism today that says that absolution by a priest is invalid if he moves a couple of yards outside the boundary of the diocese where he has permission to hear confessions.

Surely it is legalism to say that the marriage of two Catholics is no marriage at all if the local parish priest, or another priest sent by him, is not present as witness (even though the essence of marriage is a public exchange of vows).

It was legalism too that allowed priests in the thirteenth century to live with a woman provided they paid a "whore tax";[18] it was legalism that in our time allowed meat on Friday in Spain, on payment of a money offering.

It is legalism that invented limbo for infants that had not had water poured on their heads—a limbo now quietly closed down again.

It is legalism today that is playing games with priests' lives and declaring their children bastards by withholding dispensations even after years of marriage.

However, in fairness it must be said that today some canon lawyers are in the forefront of change. In some instances they are even ahead of theologians and bishops, even if there are still others who remain steeped in legalism.

Clericalism, too, leads to antifeminism. The clerical caste is notorious for its hostility to women. This ranges from the quite pathetic banning of females from serving mass, to the refusal even to discuss the ordination of women, to the Cow Syndrome mentioned earlier, where women are used sexually and then discarded for the sake of the institution.

There is still the exclusion of women from any power position whatsoever outside of convents. There is still the totally male domination of the Catholic Church, where males make the rules even in what concerns women most intimately. This is sexism: It is rooted deep in the need to defend celibacy and has a long clerical history. It goes as far back as St. John Chrysostom, who said in the fourth century, "Among all savage beasts, none is found as harmful as woman," and St. Thomas Aquinas, who said in the thirteenth century, "Woman is defective and accidental . . . a male gone awry . . . the result of some weakness in the father's generative power."

Sexism has been roundly condemned by U.S. bishops Balke and Lucker in a 1981 pastoral letter: "When anyone believes that men are inherently superior to women . . . then he or she is guilty of sexism. Sexism is a moral and social evil. It is not the truth of the biological, sociological or psychological sciences, nor is it the truth of the Gospel. Sexism is a lie. It is a grievous sin, diminished in its gravity only by indeliberate ignorance or by pathological fear."[19]

The sexism of the clerical caste is of course rejected by many priests. Some have left because of it. Others have stayed and formed an international group to combat clerical sexism. Called Priests for Equality, the group has publicly asked pardon of the Church's women, adding: "Our personal apologies for the gender discrimination of our Church cannot remedy the hurt and anger which you feel when a community that proclaims its following of Christ clings to discriminatory, authoritarian and patriarchal structures that violate the spirit and witness of Jesus. We understand, in our own way, the feelings which might urge you to leave the community and seek other, less painful, ways of worshipping God."[20]

Clericalism does much of its thinking purely from theory, deducing from first principles, without putting it to the test of experience. It then imposes its conclusions on ordinary people, trying to control their behavior in ways that their everyday experience tells them are wrong. Thus we find a celibate male clericalism dictating what behavior should or should not take place in the bedroom, which would be funny if it were not for the misery it causes.

The clerical caste is also steeped in gnosticism, one of the oldest and most persistent of all heresies, which sees the body as evil and only the spirit as good. It results in a hang-up about people taking their clothes off, instead of a concern for putting clothes on those who have none, which is what mattered to Christ.

The hang-up can reach ludicrous levels, as in 1987 when a married man, Ivo Schmitt, was ordained in Brazil by special Vatican permission. Before his ordination, Schmitt was required to sign a Vatican document vowing to refrain from intercourse; his wife, Adulina, also signed papers renouncing her rights as wife, although they would continue to live in the same house. It's called Living as Brother and Sister. After the ordination, Adulina was heard to say, "From now on, all he gets from me is kisses."

What does this say but that sex is dirty?

One of the results of this fear of sexuality, according to Richard Sipe, is that the Catholic Church has failed to develop a credible theology of sexuality. Sipe calls it the "black hole" in Christian theology, which has been made more and more obvious by progress in psychology, medicine, and clinical and pastoral experience. This, again, is basic to priests' leaving: Celibacy is hard enough to live at the best of times, but harder still when its theological basis becomes doubtful, and when one suspects it is really about clerical control of one's life.

Clericalism is surrounded by an infinitely subtle hinting that its members are not quite fully men. Ordinary people are well aware of this: It shows in their expectation that the "good" boy, the gentle or studious boy, the boy who is not interested in girls, becomes the priest. Docility is even one of the criteria for accepting seminarians in some institutions. For most priests, this subtle hinting is hard to bear. They sometimes react by being extremely macho, or by becoming superb sportsmen.

This sexual ambivalence, an inevitable spin-off of compulsory celibacy, is one of the most repulsive characteristics of clerical life. It is also undoubtedly what drives men to leave the clerical condition, for many of the reasons given for leaving can be boiled down to precisely this.

It was a Brazilian, Eduardo Hoornaert, who made me realize that clericalism is a purely European phenomenon and quite out of place, and even offensive, in certain other cultures. "It's a Roman import," he told me. "As a clerical structure the Church is purely European. For Europeans, the Church is principally the clerical institution. But for us, especially for the Indians, the Church is the *povo* ('the people'). The people of God."

In trying to force clerical structures on Brazilians—structures such as celibacy, Roman legalism, European-style hierarchy—the Vatican is committing the same crime as any colonial power—forcing its customs and mores on the natives.

And it will fail, as the colonial powers did.

Fr. Bernard Häring, in a lecture in São Paulo, Brazil, in December 1987, denounced what he called "the irritating history of the sacred alliance between the throne and the altar: a hierarchical and clerical church pleased to get wealth, honors and privileges from the powerful for favoring an unequal order which enriched the wealthy few at the expense of the impoverished masses."[21] That is clericalism at its ugliest and most blatant.

These are the things that priests are renouncing when they leave. Almost all the reasons cited by priests for leaving can be

reduced to one or another aspect of clericalism: vows growing mean-
ingless as a community ceases to challenge society; kids' eating
from priests' garbage cans; forced resignation after having denounced military parades and having said that poverty was not
wished by God but by rulers and oppressors—all these have to do
with a clericalism facing toward Mammon and away from the people of God.

Priests who leave because they feel trapped, or because they
feel excluded from human life, or because they feel perceived as
sexually ambivalent, are breaking out of clerical apartness. Those
who leave from loneliness or for love are doing the same, or are re-
acting against that great bulwark of clericalism—enforced celibacy.

Priests who leave over the ban on contraception are instinc-
tively rejecting clericalism's way of putting people's basic needs
last, and the institution's survival first.

Lately such priests are finding how accurate their instincts
were, for it is now revealed that the ban on contraception was
renewed in 1968 (against an overwhelming vote in the Papal Commission on Birth Control) precisely because Cardinal Ottaviani
warned the pope in a letter that a change in teaching might under-
mine the credibility of the institution and endanger confidence in
Church teaching.[22] So credibility was allowed to outweigh the desperate need of millions throughout the world. Ironically, it was this
action that brought the greatest loss of credibility in several centuries.

In the prologue I wrote of the lack of an accurate term for
priests who leave. They are not "apostates," as they have not left
the Church. They are not "ex-priests" or "former priests," as most
have not left priesthood or ministry. But I think they would gladly
accept the term "ex-cleric," or "non-clerical priest."

It is not only priests who leave who reject clericalism. Some of
the most eminent churchmen also do so. Fr. Leonardo Boff calls for
the emergence of "another form of being church," as opposed to
"the expansion of an existing ecclesiastical system, rotating on a
. . . clerical axis."[23]

"Think," says the theologian Fr. Yves Congar, "of the
church as a huge organization, controlled by a hierarchy, with
subordinates whose only task is to keep the rules and follow the
practices. Would this be a caricature? Scarcely."[24] But it would
be clericalism.

Bishop Kalilombe, in an African context, speaks of "what should be called clericalism, that is, the sorry fact that basic ministry and effective leadership and responsibility are concentrated unduly on only the ordained type of ministry."[25]

When I think of clericalism I think of the famous Greek sculpture, the Laocoön, in which a father and his sons are engaged in a struggle to the death with loathsome serpents, the coils of which are entwining thighs and locking arms and torsos and tightening inexorably upon throats. Aptly enough that sculpture is in the Vatican.

Yet it would be a mistake, I believe, to see clericalism as some sort of wicked "them," as opposed to a noble and upright "us." Clericalism may be a structure, but it is also a state of mind, like Phariseeism, and the virus is in all of us. We relapse into it whenever we put power and control before the service of God's people, and even laypeople, members of confraternities and knights, are capable of that. Jesus told us not to lord it like the pagans, but to be the servant of all. His washing of those feet was the ultimate gesture against clericalism.

Anyhow, the Laocoön may be in the Vatican, but the Holy Spirit is there too, as everywhere else in the Church. And we were promised that the Gates of Hell would not prevail.*

All human things degenerate, even the human side of the Church, and are in constant need of renewal. But our faith tells us, and history demonstrates, that the Church has some extraordinary power of self-renewal.

Perhaps that is what we are seeing now, as clericalism starts to crack. It is being assailed on all sides. The clerical attitude to women

---

* Theologian Heinz-Jürgen Vogels disagrees with my hypothesis that clericalism is the root cause of priests leaving the ministry. He says the root cause is compulsory celibacy and nothing else. I paraphrase here a letter he wrote to me after reading this chapter. "The charism [gift] of celibacy is not given by God to every priest, so that many of them are simply 'incapable' of celibacy, though definitely called by God to the priesthood. Here we have the most simple, most general and most convincing explanation of the failure of celibacy throughout history and plainly in our times: vocation to priesthood and vocation to celibacy are not identical and do not always coincide. The Second Vatican Council took over this reasoning and states explicitly three things: (1) 'Celibacy is a *gift* from God.' (2) 'Celibacy is *not required* by the essence of priesthood,' and (3) thus you can only 'pray that God may generously grant this gift to all obliged priests' (Presb. Ord. No. 16). This implies that you can no longer demand it from all priests. This is not your or my personal opinion, but the one of the Church. It is *the* 'root cause,' explaining both the success of celibate priests who stay, and the impossibility of celibacy for so many others who leave."

is being met by a powerful feminism: As woman's status rises, it becomes harder and harder to see her as the medieval temptress, the Eve to be guarded against. And as woman takes her full place in society, she is demanding it too in Church.

Mutual love and support now have equal status with procreation as the purpose of marriage, and marriage is no longer seen as inferior to celibacy. So the clerical downgrading of sex is being confronted, and priests everywhere are asking what is the justification for enforced celibacy, or are simply rejecting it, either by ignoring its demands or by leaving to marry.

Liberation theology and the "option for the poor" has led many ground-level clerics to look again at their role. This is especially true when they are ordered to stay out of politics, whereas the higher clerics are seen as deeply involved in politics, too often on the side of the right-wing big battalions.

And the old cruel legalism is being more and more ignored: As one priest put it, the Curia is still pushing the buttons, but the lights aren't going on anymore.

The priests are crying out for freedom, that freedom that clericalism took from them. Another of those Vatican II documents, prepared for the council bishops by a *peritus,* and still marked "Secret," bears out the reality of this cry for freedom.[26] One of the main problems of the priest today, it says, is a sense of alienation. He feels he has lost his place in modern society. In older societies he felt needed, his education was valued, his theology was accepted. The modern world values him less; he feels no longer adapted, that he has little to offer. The fact that he is not free to participate in the workplace, rear a family, or share in normal burdens and anxieties, increases this alienation.

Family life, and the need to go out and work to support a family, would be an antidote to such alienation. Many priests have sought the freedom to do just these things.

But meanwhile, back at the Vatican, for the moment clericalism still rules. Priests and people around the world, and even some bishops and cardinals, are well aware of the lengthening cracks in the clerical mold, but that awareness has not yet penetrated the Vatican.

Those great Bernini colonnades in front of St. Peter's had always seemed to me a symbol of the Church, arms open to embrace the world. Now when I think of the Vatican, I no longer see those arms embracing the world, but the high dark walls. Not Vatican City but Vatican Citadel. Inside are men of goodwill, some of goodness, some perhaps even of holiness. Yet you could hammer on those walls until kingdom come, and no one would hear you.

CHAPTER 10

The Gathering

Take care what you do with these men. . . . For if this plan or this undertaking is of men, it will fail; but if it is of God, you will not be able to overthrow them. You might even be found opposing God.

Acts 5:35–39

LITTLE Sybille, a child of a German priest who has not acknowledged her, trots across to her Mutti—a slender, young woman who is a respected attorney. Mutti lifts her on to her shoulders, and Sybille surveys the scene, her eyes wide as saucers.

She is gazing out over the flat roof of the Casa della CGIL, a trade union building in Ariccia, set high in the cool hills outside Rome. The pope might almost hear the singing, as his Castel Gandolfo residence is just about on the other side of the hill. It is August 27, 1987, and this is the closing mass of the worldwide congress of the International Federation of Catholic Married Priests and Their Partners.

Well over one hundred have traveled here from Germany, South Africa, Britain, Argentina, Austria, Belgium, Canada, Brazil, Spain, the United States, France, Holland, Ireland, Italy, the Philippines, and Czechoslovakia. Argentina is represented by an outspoken bishop, Jeronimo Podestà, with his wife, Clelia. Not all the priests are married, of course, and there are also some active diocesan and religious order priests from Spain and Italy.

It has been a week of prayer, planning, debate, resolutions, and sharing, with the world's press and television giving a surprising amount of coverage. It is also the week in which this worldwide movement—in its self-confidence and in the maturity of its resolutions—has come of age.

Only a few decades ago the priests who left were the *Desaparecidos* ("Disappeared ones") of the Roman Catholic Church. Their role was of solitary, shuffling pariahs, of whom Christian society asked only that they disappear off the face of the earth. And disappear they did, not only into anonymity, but into an aloneness that engulfed even the women courageous enough to share their lives.

The old ways can take a while to die. Yet everywhere they are yielding to a new phenomenon: All over the world the ex-clerics are emerging from their purdah to take their rightful place in their Church. They are forming organizations that will speak for them to the people of God and to Church authorities if these will listen, and where they can support and help each other.

Organization often begins when the married and resigned priests of an area start to cluster in small local groups, such as Connections in Texas and Louisiana or the Social Umbrella in Oregon, and has evolved to the point where many countries now have national organizations of ex-clerics, their wives, and families. Some of these organizations have acquired considerable clout.

Most groups share certain principal aims—mutual support of the members, spiritual, emotional, and physical; help in finding employment; liaison with the people and with Church authorities; consciousness-raising in the Church by putting the case for optional celibacy and a married priesthood; working toward a renewal of all forms of ministry in the Church.

Some groups are loose enough to include everyone, from those who long to return to formal ministry to those who would never dream of doing so.

Why are such groups emerging at this particular time? One reason is that people didn't have time until now. For many priests who left, those first years were usually a struggle to hold down a job and make a family. It is only now, with children growing up, with perhaps some security achieved, that they are beginning to get time to do things.

There seems to be a kind of evolutionary process in these groups of resigned priests. In the early stages, all they can do is share their feelings and talk, perhaps for the first time, of their hurts and anger. Then there is a veteran's reunion stage, with the usual recollections of boot camp. Then the wives start coming to the fore, and there is emphasis on helping those in hard times. Then comes the high-profile stage: invitations from the media for interviews, with a will-I-or-won't-I-go-public dilemma. Many individuals decide to go public, and with that comes a euphoric sense of walking tall. From then on comes a new confidence in the whole group, and the group finds itself functioning partly as a lobby.

A striking example of an effective lobbying group is the Corpus organization in the United States. Corpus explicitly promotes the aim of optional celibacy and a married priesthood in the Catholic Church, including the return to full ministry of those who had to resign to marry. Its members declare their willingness to resume such ministry.

Corpus began back in 1974 when a U.S. bishop declared that priests who resign and marry have no further interest in the Church. At that time there were ten thousand such priests. In Chicago two married priests, Frank Bonnike and Frank McGrath, replied that a great many such men would dearly love to serve the Church again, even in an active role as priests.

That same year the National Opinion Research Center (NORC) conducted a nationwide survey which indicated that 79 percent of Catholics would prefer a married priest as their pastor. Encouraged by all this, Bonnike, McGrath, and two other Chicago married priests founded Corpus—Corps of Reserve Priests United for Service.

During the next ten years the four Corpus facilitators asked three thousand resigned priests if they would be willing to function again—in a situation analagous to the reserve corps in the military. About one thousand said yes, and this pattern of one third saying yes has been consistently repeated in the intervening years.

Corpus is now in its sixteenth year: The organization has grown to be a powerful voice in the U.S. Catholic Church, with over four thousand members, a mailing list of eight thousand for the bimonthly *Corpus Report,* unofficial financial support from some of the bishops, and a highly professional approach to the media.

Corpus's full-time national coordinator, Dr. Terence Dosh, is a former Benedictine monk.

He is the first to point out that Corpus still has a long way to go. The number of resigned priests in the United States has now risen to eighteen thousand, and it will be a formidable task to locate and make contact with many of them. Nevertheless, Dosh travels relentlessly in an effort to do this.

When further change finally comes to the Catholic Church, in the matter of ministry, priesthood, and celibacy, Corpus will certainly have had something to do with it, if only because it is a huge and effective operation in the most powerful province of the Catholic Church. Things happen earlier in the Americas, both North and South, and they rattle Rome's cage more—simply because what happens in the American Church today happens in the World Church tomorrow.

There are now national or nationwide organizations of resigned/ married priests in Germany, Austria, Belgium (two separate groups), Spain (three groups), France (three groups), Italy (three groups), Ireland, Great Britain, Holland, Portugal, Switzerland, Czechoslovakia, the United States, Brazil, Argentina, Colombia, Haiti, Canada, Malta, Sri Lanka, Puerto Rico, El Salvador, Chile, South Africa, and the Philippines.

The tenor of these national organizations understandably reflects the countries of origin. Belgium, as mentioned, predictably, has two groups—one French-speaking, the other Flemish. A Spanish group, CO.SA.RE.SE. is engaged in an energetic campaign to have the years of active priesthood count toward retirement pension, as many of its members face an old age of poverty. From the bishops the campaigners have so far had "fine words, but nothing effective." Now they are talking with the state's *defensor del pueblo* ("public defender").[1]

Brazil's group, MPC–Rumos, has a good working relationship with some of the country's hierarchy, including Cardinals Arns and Lorscheider, both of whom have attended the group's meetings. Bishop Luciano Mendes, the president of the country's hierarchy, on returning from Rome in 1987 held a conference with Rumos members to brief them on developments. Cardinal Lorscheider has set aside an office in his seminary for the use of Rumos.

The atmosphere is considerably different in Holland. There the national organization, Union of Married and Unmarried Priests (called GOP), is inclined to be confrontational toward bishops, and especially toward Rome, as most Dutch Catholics are.

The Irish group arose almost spontaneously, out of what must have been a long-felt and crying need. When Corpus's Terry Dosh came to Dublin, a couple of public meetings were called to hear him, and listeners were asked if they wanted to form a resigned and married priest group. In no time there was a president, a secretary, and a lively association which called itself Leaven.

Great Britain's national group is called Advent. It traces its origins to 1969, when a group of married priests in the Midlands began getting together. Fr. Conrad Pepler, against the wishes of some bishops, lent them Spode House, a Dominican conference center and retreat house. These meetings, which included the families, were for spiritual sharing and prayer, and led eventually to the formation of a national association.

The Italian penchant for left- and right-wing polarization is reflected in Italy's two main national groups, Vocatio and ORMA. There is now also a fledgling third group, Hoc Facite. Gianni Gennari is the president of Vocatio, undoubtedly the most assertive of the groups. It now has three thousand members, of which one thousand are resigned priests and the rest spouses, priests still in active ministry, and supportive laypeople.

Vocatio is hardly a comfortable association: Its handbook calls it a "disturbing and critical voice, sharing with all men and women of goodwill the hunger and thirst for justice." Vocatio has little interest in reinstating married priests in the Church as it is but looks for a new kind of church based on liberation theology and new concepts of ministry.

Gianni Gennari, a onetime university professor of moral theology in Rome and now a journalist, is probably one of Italy's most influential married priests by virtue of the acerbic and quite brilliant column he writes in the *Paese Sera* newspaper. He has been writing it for years, since long before he left the ministry to marry in 1982. Little escapes Gennari's eye, and few high ecclesiastics are safe from his acidic pen. Not even Pope John Paul II, who, Gennari maintains, sometimes reads the column.

Again and again he returns to the themes of optional celibacy, justice for married priests, and justice for women. In the eighteenth century the Church lost the intellectuals, he said in one column. In the nineteenth century, it lost the workers. And in the twentieth century it is well on the way to losing the women.[2]

The Vocatio people have little time for ORMA, which they

regard as far too conservative, content with the Church as it is, and wanting only to have married priests ministering in an unchanged Church. "More papal than the pope," a Vocatio member growls.

ORMA is the group's popular name (taken from its bulletin title, *ORdinatio-MAtrimonio*). Its full name is the Union of Catholic Family Priests (USFC). Its members have their own misgivings about Vocatio. ORMA's founder, Paolo Camellini, speaks concernedly of the danger of "stepping outside Catholic orthodoxy." "If you don't recognize the Church hierarchy," he tells me, "if you say that the pope and bishops don't matter, if you question whether ordination is a sacrament, you're in danger of making a *chiesa acefala* ['a headless church'].

"Whereas we say, of course we want to renew this Church, but let's stay faithful to the Catholic Church that Christ founded. I mean, the pope as successor to Peter; the bishops as successors to the Apostles; unchangeable dogma. We want to renew *this* church, not to make another one, not even a better one. No, if we wanted to do any of that, we could have become Protestants.

"What we're looking for is pastoral reform, not reform of dogma."

As he tells me this, we are sitting in the summer twilight by the window of the Camellini apartment in the old part of Reggio Emilia. Directly across the street are the massive renaissance windows of the bishop's palace and offices.

Paolo Camellini is a smallish man, in his late fifties, with dark curly hair. He is gentle, not angry, even though he works as a laborer in a plastics factory. Carla, his wife, has been in the next room all afternoon, sewing a wedding dress. She does it for a living. Their little boy with Down's syndrome takes us by the hand to lead us in to supper.

Carla serves the meal. She is rather tall, well-groomed, friendly, and matter-of-fact. She could be in her forties, but says she is older. Carla is charismatic. She says that for eighteen years Jesus has talked to her during prayer. Fr. Conrad Baisi, a seminary professor and theologian, was her spiritual adviser and studied her case for ten years. He thought her charisma was similar to that of Teresa of Avila.

Don Paolo Camellini was parish priest of a mountain village in the Apennines, where Carla used to take her two children for holidays before she was widowed. She knew Don Paolo only slightly.

One day Carla went to Don Paolo and told him she had had a revelation that they should get married, so as to dedicate themselves to the cause of married priests. Jesus had told her that he wanted married priests, but only in holiness—"holy as priests, and holy as spouses."

Carla says, "Paolo was devoted to his celibate life. He actually cried when this was presented to him. He loved his role. But he wrote out his request to marry and brought the documents to the bishop.

"He was called to Rome and asked why he wanted to marry. Paulo replied, 'Because this woman says Jesus asked her to marry me.'

"One month later came the dispensation from Rome."

There is silence around the supper table. The little boy reaches over and pats my arm. I ask what were Jesus's exact words.

"Jesus said, 'Do not fear this choice because it is a spot of oil that grows always bigger, and that no one can ever stop. I wanted this mission for a renewed Church. Because too much blood has been poured out for this my work in you.' "

Carla pauses. "That last bit frightened me," she says. "I thought of past cruelties, of abandoned kids of priests, maybe. Or of the priests who have perhaps died or killed themselves. I still don't fully understand the meaning of those last words."

I turn to Paolo. Did he believe all this at the time, I ask him.

Paolo answers, "Yes, I did. I had always loved my celibacy. I had always lived it and had never once betrayed it. But I understood, I am a child of God, and God can do with me whatever He wants. I said to God, 'I once offered you my celibacy. Now you want me to marry. *Va bene.*' "

They married in 1970, and they are convinced their subsequent history shows the hand of God. In 1979 they met Giustino Zampini (who had resigned and married over fifty years before, suffering frightful privations in those days), and together they founded ORMA.

In 1980 the Camellinis began working on an international gathering of married priests. It took place at Chiusi in 1983, bringing together married priests mostly from Europe, and for the first time in history.

This of course was the beginning of the most remarkable development in the whole saga of resigned and married priests. For years thousands of resigned priests had lived in isolation. Then suddenly all over the world, almost spontaneously, they began to cluster into groups.

But for some years, those groups themselves were isolated, each thinking it was the only one in the world, not realizing that it was part of something happening simultaneously in many countries of the world. Then came the gathering at Chiusi, the word spread, and the groups around the world found themselves saying, "We are not alone." Other international gatherings were to follow.

How did the Camellinis get the idea of that first international synod?

Carla said, "Jesus told me it was time to go out and talk to everybody, in any way possible. Like at Pentecost. At that moment Paolo was down in the courtyard, praying, walking up and down. Suddenly he got an idea—let's start an international gathering. He came up and told me. We talked and decided to call it a synod. Later we suggested it in the ORMA bulletin. Then the press took it up. . . ."

The Chiusi synod was followed by another synod in 1985, this time held at Ariccia, outside Rome. It led to the setting up of an International Federation of Married Priest Groups. This federation, headquartered in Paris, has gone on to bring worldwide recognition to the movement. Bert Peeters, a Belgian, is its president, and Pierre and Micheline Lautrey of Paris are the movement's secretaries.

In 1987 came the International Congress of Married Priests and Partners, also held at Ariccia. And in the summer of 1990 another international congress was held, this time in Holland just twelve miles from Amsterdam.

The gatherings so far have been seen as milestones in the movement toward a married priesthood and a renewed ministry. Each has had its own particular flavor and emphasis, as experience accumulates, thinking matures, and goals are refined.

The 1985 Synod at Ariccia concentrated on the desirability of a married priesthood and produced a schema of the biblical, historical, and theological data that support the compatibility of the two sacraments of matrimony and ordination to the priesthood. The synod stressed that the heart of the Church's problem is a defective attitude toward marriage and sexuality, and a narrow attitude to priesthood: A priest is not primarily someone who gives up marriage, but a ministering person who gives himself to others, spouse and children included. And it became clear during the session that some bishops around the world had encouraged married priests to attend, some even paying travel and accommodations for them and their families.

The Vatican's attitude was made explicit in a meeting in which three of the synod's coordinators, Paolo Camellini, Fr. Lambert Van Gelder, and Heinz-Jürgen Vogels, met with Monsignor Canciani, the unofficial mediator appointed from the Vatican's Congregation of the Clergy. The following observations are from a report on that meeting by the three synod representatives:

1. The Congregation does not want to treat us as a group or organization, but only with individuals, about each personal case. (This is the old advice: *Divide et impera* ["divide and conquer"].)

2. They have got "quite precise instructions" from the Vatican Secretary of State, Cardinal Casaroli—Canciani said—"not to give you status or an official character" (*non dare importanza, non dare ufficialità*).

3. We would have the right to gather as a civilian corps, like a trade union, but we are, for them, "outside of the Church" (*fuori della Chiesa*). It seems they mean: "outside the clergy." The expression tells much about the conception of Church that the Congregation has.

4. If they would give way to us, Canciani said, everything would break down (*crollerebbe tutto*), because it is a matter of principle. Probably they mean: the priestly celibate discipline would break down (the Church itself cannot break down from married priests, since there are already such in East and West. It shows that there are irrational fears behind the attitude).

5. They perceive a "convergent strategy" working in different initiatives throughout the world, said Canciani (strangely enough they do not observe that all those spontaneous movements cannot have been started by one man, but must originate finally from the Spirit) . . .

6. We should not expect the Congregation to speak, Canciani said. We, however, should speak ourselves and give a testimony of a "historical faith" and a "lived faith" (*fede storica e fede vissuta*), which means a faith that respects the grown tradition and which is active in our new condition of life

(this is exactly what we are doing in our documents: they are historically proving our claim to minister as married priests and speak of the present life of the priests in their communities). It appears that with this testimony of faith they would accept us as full members of the Church, or would even expect a changing of the situation (which was not actually said, but why else should they expect such a testimony from us?).

Monsignor Canciani added by himself: Even the Roman congregations are groaning under the present general "stagnation"—they "only repeat what has been said ever since, without uttering anything new." But: "When doors are closed, all mouths are open" *(A porte chiuse, tutte bocche sono aperte)*.[3]

By the time the next international gathering was due—the Ariccia Congress of 1987—a considerable evolution in thinking had taken place. Two schools of thought were developing within the national groups preparing for the congress: whether to concentrate simply on pressing for a married priesthood and optional celibacy, or whether to work toward a far wider renewal of the concept of ministry in the Church.

The differences were spelled out among Britain's married priests when the Scot Joe Mulrooney, provoked by a preliminary questionnaire circulated by the congress organizers, passed around a paper of his own entitled "Some Reflections on the Forthcoming Congress." Then to this Adrian Hastings made answer with his "Comment upon 'Some Reflections.' "[4]

Mulrooney attacked the precongress preoccupation with abolishing compulsory celibacy as "inward turned and too concerned with its own affairs. Not all left for reasons of celibacy," he said. "There are many other motives . . . and we can lump them all together under the term 'institutional incompatibility.' The congress must take the whole picture on board, or its documentation will read like a Roman document, in seeing marriage as the only reason for leaving."

Not everyone aspires to return to priesthood in the sense of a full sacramental ministry, Joe Mulrooney said. "Many aspire to fulfill their 'mission' vocation, or indeed are already doing so, in a variety of roles other than the sacramental."

He said the congress organizers had lost touch with whole areas of ministry and responsibility stemming directly from baptism rather than from ordination; they had lost touch with the emergence of a committed laity to perform such ministries, a laity no longer content to be passive and subject to the clerical caste as sole repositories of authority.

As for the ministry of the sacraments, Mulrooney called for a study of "how we find, train, and ordain" its ministers. Should they be chosen by the community itself? "The autocratic imposition on a community of someone (be he celibate or married) from outside the community, will no longer suffice."

Outside of this broader context, Mulrooney insisted, the question of "Priesthood, married or celibate" is just a red herring. "If we simply adopt as our aim, in isolation, the abolition of the law of celibacy, we will appear to outsiders simply as a self-serving group, seeking its own interests."

In reply, Adrian Hastings conceded that the congress's preparatory materials "clearly did not point toward a far wider reform of the ministry," and it would be far from satisfactory simply to have married priests ministering in an unchanged Church.

But, he said, it is a matter of tactics. "It would be far, far easier to change other aspects of priestly ministry *if* this one great change were made—'the abolition of the law of celibacy for all secular priests.' It is that law that has imposed rigidity all across the board, that so divides clergy from laity, professionals from the rest, etc. And, being grossly unjust, it has led to lots of other related injustices."

Anyway, said Hastings, the law of compulsory celibacy is far from a red herring. "Deep down, the law has itself produced one context, and its abolition will *ipso facto* go very far to abolishing that context: It will immediately allow and encourage, especially in many third world countries, a radical alteration in the shape of the ministry, for example, in regard to basic communities. . . .

"It is not true that the celibacy issue in itself is just a red herring. It is, on the contrary, the major point at which the Roman tradition went wrong. It is unscriptural, indeed antiscriptural, deeply unjust, and immensely wide in its impact upon past and present.

"It also has the sheer clarity, in terms of theology, law, spirituality, and pastoral need, which make it a very good point to target."

These two positions, clearly defined, ran like threads through the congress. A consensus gradually emerged, where people began to realize that compulsory celibacy, while perhaps not a red herring, was far from being the whole picture.

The two threads, optional celibacy or a totally renewed ministry, became the warp and the woof of discussion. It became clear that since the previous synod, many of the delegates had found new ways to minister, without waiting for a nod from Rome. And their whole concept of ministry was expanding vastly.

The Belgian Jesuit Fr. Jan Kerkhofs, a sociologist, rector of a college in Louvain, and head of the Pro Mundi Vita Institute, gave what amounted to a keynote address to the assembly. More than half of all Christian ministers, he said, are married men and women. The Latin rite is the exception. He spoke of the rapid evolution of new forms of ministry, and of a move away from the pyramid structure of the Church. The new idea of Church is of concentric circles, with the pope and hierarchy in the middle rather than on top, and where service rather than tyranny prevails.

With nearly half the world's parishes now without a priest, unless there is some change, there will be *no* church left in the third world. Bishops from all around the world are telling Rome this and begging to be allowed married priests. Priest councils everywhere in Europe are likewise asking for change.

The theology of priesthood and ministry is evolving, Kerkhofs said. Theologians stress that ministers and leaders should be drawn from the community, rather than sent in from outside; that ministry could be temporary, and not necessarily concerned about sacramental character. And there is *no* first-rank theologian today who says women should not be ordained.

It is women, in fact, who will change the whole Church in the coming years, more than cardinals or bishops. If they are not allowed to, Kerkhofs fears, they will leave the Church, and take their children with them.

We should always talk of ministry rather than priesthood, he counseled—ministry that can be either sacramental or nonsacramental: ministry of the sacraments or of service.

The most effective way to change attitudes is by the good example and credibility of married priest groups, Fr. Kerkhofs said. Individual bishops will begin to trust these priests and will invite them to take on pastoral care (precisely as is happening in Brazil).

It is no use trying to contact Rome: Rome is hopeless. When

pressed on this point, Kerkhofs was adamant: Rome is hopeless. He knows his history and has dealt much with Rome. Leave Rome alone, he said, and spend your energy locally or nationally. Support your own bishops, especially those who go out on a limb, and give courage to the slower ones to move.

Prof. Kerkhofs—no wild man of the Catholic Church but a distinguished Jesuit—believes there will be married priests in ten years and women priests in twenty.

In the end, what emerged from the week's discussions was a consciousness that life after leaving was not about sitting around, waiting for Rome to do something or permit something, like the scriptural handmaiden with her eye on the hand of her mistress. As one delegate put it, there's no need to tilt at Vatican windmills, like Don Quixote. "Let's be more like Sancho Panza, bypassing the snapping curial sails, and plod serenely forward." Let us do whatever ministry we can, and let the Holy Spirit take care of optional celibacy and married priesthood.

It was a few days after the congress ended that I went to see Don Franzoni, the former abbot of St. Paul's, and he said almost the same thing. He earnestly cautioned against concentrating efforts solely on attaining optional celibacy. "I don't believe in the liberation of the priest outside the liberation of man," he said. "A church that struggles for liberation, that fights racism, exploitation of women, apartheid, will take on a new shape. It will have a wider horizon, will be a Church of service, not of power.

"And within that process there will also be resolved the question of married priests and celibacy. It will happen en route." Seek first the Kingdom of God, and all these will be added.

"Most important, and hardest, is to be a believer, to become a disciple of Jesus. But in a church of such disciples, will it matter who has the gift of tongues, who presides at the Eucharist?"

CHAPTER 11

Celibacy, Forced or Free?

For it has seemed good to the Holy Spirit and to us to lay upon you no greater burden than these necessary things.

Acts:15, 28

TRUE celibacy, freely chosen (or freely accepted) for the Kingdom of God, is a many-splendored thing in man or woman. And it is one of the easiest things to discern: You know it by the love it generates. One would surely see it in Mother Teresa, in Dom Helder Camara, in Cardinal Lorscheider, in Brother Roger of Taize. One would have seen it in Gandhi, in Pope John XXIII, in Dorothy Day, in Padre Pio. I encountered it in a nun who was a hospital matron; in a man who once taught me; in certain priests who were my colleagues; and in some priests whom I lately met in missionary lands. There is a translucence about such people, and a goodness and energy that are unmistakable.

Psychologists suggest that such goodness and energy comes from the deepest roots of sexuality. In an address to the National Guild of Catholic Psychiatrists on May 8, 1988, Richard Sipe quoted Eknath Easwaran on Gandhi:

158

It was in South Africa that Gandhi learned to translate . . . tremendous ideals into effective action. . . . Night and day, carrying . . . stretchers across the vast deserted hill country of Natal, he plunged himself deep into prayer and self-examination in a fervent search for greater strength with which to serve.

The intensity of his desire led him to the source of power itself. Deep in meditation Gandhi began to see how much of his vital energy was locked up in the sexual desire. In a flood of insight he realized that sex is not just a physical instinct, but an expression of the tremendous spiritual force behind all love and creativity which the Hindu scriptures call *kundalini*, the life-force of evolution. All his life it had been his master, buffeting him this was and that beyond his control. But in the silence of the Natal hills, with all his burning desire to serve focussed by weeks of tending to the wounded and dying, Gandhi found the strength to tap his power at its source. Then and there he resolved to be its master, and never to let it dictate to him again. It was a decision which resolved his deepest tensions, and released all the love within him into his conscious control. He had begun to transform the last of his passions into spiritual power.[1]

Such free celibacy serves a very special purpose in a priest who is so endowed. Frs. Gallagher and Vandenberg in their book *The Celibacy Myth* point out that celibacy does not just free the priest for more duties. The unique thing about priesthood, they suggest, is not just service or ministry: "What a priest has to offer his people, that no one else has to offer, is the unique relationship he can have with them as their priest. Just as a couple's activity takes on a deeper significance and even a new meaning to the degree that there is genuine commitment and bonding between them, so priestly activity becomes truly 'priestly' to the degree that it reflects a genuine commitment and bonding between himself and his people.

"Enter celibacy. As a catalyst speeds up and enhances the chemical reaction of two elements without being essential to that reaction, the charism of celibacy deepens and enhances the relationship of the priest with his people, without being essential to that relationship."[2]

And that is what we perceive in a priest who is truly gifted with celibacy. Such a gift, by the way, need not mean ease—it could involve day-to-day struggle, and reiterated choice, as with Gandhi. Celibacy is not bachelorhood, or simply a contentment with solitude. If it is a charism, as some maintain—then a charism is a gift from God, not for oneself, but for the benefit of others. Like the gift of tongues. It does not have to be comfortable.

"You don't just promise celibacy on the day you become a deacon," Cardinal Hume explained to me in an interview. "You have to renew it every day. Profoundly I believe in the two creation chapters of Genesis, in which we are told to increase and multiply, and that it is not good for man to be alone. Now celibacy is saying *no* to both of those—it can only do that if it is saying yes to something else. To being open to the love which you come to understand in God, and through that, to try and give love to all the people you are involved with."

It is that love that bonds the celibate priest to his people as few things can.

A celibacy, however, that is externally and indiscriminately forced upon every priest, whether willing or not, whether capable of it or not, is light-years from the celibacy I just described.

And such compulsory celibacy has rather strange origins in history. Let us take a brief look at a few moments in that history, bearing in mind the dangers of oversimplification, and that these are indeed but moments in a long and complicated evolution extending across twelve hundred or more years. But Cardinal Doepfner did warn the Fathers of the Second Vatican Council that they should try to know something of celibacy's history before making decisions about it.[3]

To begin with, Christ did not require celibacy of his followers and included married men among his Apostles. Neither did the Scripture that followed demand celibacy of anyone, even though it was seen as apt for the expected end of the world. St. Paul left it as a free choice ("concerning celibacy I have no commandment of the Lord"[1 Cor. 25:40]), insisting merely that ministers be "the husband of one wife."

In the three centuries that followed, there were both married and unmarried ministers. Clement of Alexandria could write: "Really also the husband of one wife is accepted by the Church, be he priest, deacon or layman, as long as he uses marriage without blame. He will take part in salvation by raising children.''

According to Edward Schillebeeckx in his book *The Church with a Human Face,* compulsory celibacy has its origins in a partly pagan notion of ritual purity.[4] First, in the fourth century came a law that forbade a married priest from having sexual intercourse the night before celebrating the Eucharist. But then the Western Church began to celebrate the Eucharist daily, so this abstinence became in fact a permanent condition for married priests.

"At the origin of the law of abstinence, and later the law of celibacy," Schillebeeckx says, "we find an antiquated anthropology and an ancient view of sexuality." At St. Jerome put it, expressing the notion of both pagans and Christians of his time: "All sexual intercourse is impure."

Understandably this obligation on married priests, to live with a wife as if she were a sister, was an intolerable burden and "led many priests into deplorable situations," as Schillebeeckx says. "These ancient councils bear abundant witness to this." So in 1139, at the Second Lateran Council, the Church resorted to drastic means: It forbade altogether the marriages of priests and declared such existing marriages null and void. The law of abstinence had become a law of celibacy. And again ritual purity was the decisive motive. "One does not approach the altar and the consecrated vessels with soiled hands"—that had been the pagan view, now enshrined by the Christians in their law of compulsory celibacy.

There were two further developments, neither of which were at the origin of the law of celibacy, but that had some influence on its consolidation.

First, more and more bishops began to be appointed from the monks, who had vows of chastity, and these gradually imposed monastic notions of virginity as suitable for all priests, even those not living in monasteries.[5]

The second development was the acquiring of property by the Church. There was a real danger that legitimate children of priests could inherit, thus depriving the Church of its property. It became critical as many of the clergy were nobles, some even royalty. Hence was a further (economic) motive for retaining celibacy for priests, since illegitimate children could not inherit.[6]

Incredible harshness was at times used to enforce the law of celibacy. The Council of Toledo in 655 decreed the enslavement of the offspring of clerics, which was incorporated into general Church law, along with the enslavement of the wives of the clerics.[7] Much later that law was put into ferocious effect under Pope Gregory VII in the eleventh century, when the marriages of priests were savagely broken up and priests' wives and children made into slaves.[8]

The 1139 celibacy law did not end matters, but in many cases merely changed marriage into concubinage. A document prepared for the bishops in the Second Vatican Council by the eminent church historian Hubert Jedin, and still marked "Secret," contains the following passage:

> As it is certain that there have always and everywhere been priests who live exemplarily, so a noticeable pro- portion, especially among the parish clergy, kept able- bodied women in their prime, when they had no blood- relations, in order to look after the housekeeping and agriculture, on which their economic existence to a large degree depended. They lived together with them and by them had children who often grew up in the vicarage. It would be a mistake to imagine that these permanent con- cubines, especially in the countryside, would have aroused a lot of scandal. We know of many cases where these "keepers of concubines" possessed the sympathies of their parishioners and were looked on as good and virtuous pastors. So they should not be judged out of hand to be simply morally unprincipled brutes. . . .
>
> The keepers of concubines were in many dioceses punished by fines and then tolerated; what is much worse is that these fines (the "whore-tax") formed a not incon- siderable source of income for the Bishop and Archdea- con. The Bishop of Luettich, Cardinal Erhard V. der Marck, frankly admits this bad state of affairs. There is solid evidence which comes from the account-books of the ecclesiastical officialates.[9]

Then came the Reformation, and the Council of Trent, by which the Roman Catholic Church reformed itself and remodeled the priest- hood to what we know today. But even then the emperor begged the council fathers to allow priests to marry. The following years proved him wise. Professor Jedin comments: "Even long after the Council of Trent, a part of the people of Switzerland ranged themselves on the side of those with concubines against Nounce Bonhomini who wanted to impose the law of celibacy in all strictness. 'Many keepers of concubines,' writes the Catholic historian Oskar Vasella, 'enjoyed the trust of the people. Despite all human failings, they carried on their care of souls in unconditional loyalty to their calling and devoted love towards their flock.' "[10]

This is backed up by Fr. Michael Pfiegler in his book *Priesterliche Existenz* (*Priestly Existence*). Even after the Council of Trent, although the law of compulsory celibacy had been promulgated with urgency, St. Clement Hofbauer found in Poland a large part of the clergy married. The situation in Latin America was no better, he says. An interesting aside is that the last Catholic bishop of Iceland was given absolution, as was his wife, before being hanged along with two of his sons by Lutherans in 1550.

But why did the Council of Trent insist on compulsory celibacy in spite of so much evidence that it could not work? Professor Jedin suggests it was an overreaction to the Protestants, who had recommended marriage for priests and had insisted that celibacy was God's gift only to a few. "Therefore the Church entrenched its position and did not let itself discuss the problem, either from the viewpoint of theology or of practical circumstances."

Remember that the preceding quotations are not from some anti-Catholic historian, but from a secret document prepared for the information of the bishops at Vatican II.

Today the law of celibacy is still with us. However, we cannot reject it merely because of its origins. Schillebeeckx points out that however peculiar those origins of celibacy are, they say nothing against its validity today. We must examine celibacy on its merits, and clearly a celibacy that is voluntarily undertaken and experienced as a charism has immense value.

But what of compulsory celibacy today? Schillebeeckx says there are only two worthwhile arguments against it. First, is it credible to people? "Now, celibate priests are constantly under the suspicion of 'wanting to marry, but not being allowed to,' as the common saying goes." Second, Christian communities have a right to leaders and to the Eucharist, and if compulsory celibacy is depriving them of such leaders, then it must be questioned. "In such a situation," he says, "Church legislation, which can in any case be changed, must give way to the more urgent right to the apostolic and eucharistic building up of the community.''

The reason, of course, that compulsory celibacy is not credible to people is that it is not seen to work today, anymore than it did in the past. In fact it seems to be unworkable.

Compulsory celibacy is in fact less workable today than ever because its original basis of ritual purity has been kicked away—by no less an agent than the Second Vatican Council. When the council proclaimed the sacredness of the marriage bond, and expressly stated that ''the actions within marriage, by which the couple are united intimately and chastely, are noble and worthy ones,''[11] it was rejecting the notion of unclean sex, sounding the death knell of the compulsory celibacy built upon it, and proclaiming that celibacy and marriage were of equal value.

Schillebeeckx has observed that ''when marriage is given its full value, and it is a sacrament, then vocations to religious celibate life will decrease.''[12] Likewise the numbers of those already celibate will decrease as thousands leave. And those who remain will demand adequate arguments for compulsory celibacy. They will not, however, get them.

I myself have heard dedicated priests asking for such arguments. One was a senior priest of the Chicago archdiocese, who asked me not to identify him. A man of mature years, he described to me in 1987 how the diocese was abandoning its ''pyjama parties''—overnight gatherings of younger priests at Mundelein Seminary, held to discuss integrating sexuality and spirituality in a priest's life. ''The groups raised so many issues,'' he told me, ''that we're going to have to scrap the rest of the pyjama parties. These young priests want a more credible explanation of celibacy, one that can reach the heart as well as the mind, and the Church's arguments are not making any sense. A guy of twenty-five is saying, 'I want to know why I'm asked to live this life-style, and if you can't convince me, do you have a right to ask me to live it?'

''We have a huge job ahead of us,'' this senior priest told me, ''and I don't think the Church can continue to say, 'Be celibate,' and not give these guys a credible rationale for remaining so.''

Many people feel like this priest: They presume that somehow, somewhere, such a credible rationale must exist. That somewhere, in some secret recess of our Church, somebody has A Reason Why, otherwise the whole Church would not still continue with compulsory celibacy—would it? Or wouldn't it? It's the old story of the Emperor's New Clothes.

The tragedy is, no such credible rationale exists. There are powerful arguments for celibacy, but they are valid for freely chosen celibacy and are not applicable to enforced celibacy. And that is why, at pajama parties or anywhere else, no one is able to come up with any. The Emperor has no clothes.

Indeed all around the world, eyes are opening to that fact. And voices, from the bottom to the top of the Catholic Church, are calling out for married priests.

As long ago as the Synod of 1971, one half of the bishops wanted a married priesthood. According to Fr. Jan Kerkhofs, the ordination of married men has been urged by the following: the national synods of Denmark, Holland, Flanders, Austria, Switzerland; the representative American congress "A Call to Action"; the Indian Congress on the Renewal of the Ministry; the colloquium of the Federation of Asian Bishops' Conferences; the combined bishops of Brazil, Bolivia, and Paraguay; the synod of Fianarantsoa in Madagascar.[13]

Likewise asking, Kerkhofs says, have been "the National Conferences of Priests in England, the United States, Zaire, South Africa; the Assembly of Provincials of the Oblates [missionary order] in Asia; the European Colloquium of Parochial Clergy; the Barcelona Assembly of Priests; the Catholic Aymaras in Peru with support from their bishops; the bishops of Chad, Cameroon, the Central Africa Empire; and so on."

The same request has been made, privately to the pope, by the Union of General Superiors of religious orders, including the heads of the Dominicans, the Franciscans, and the Jesuits.[14]

These voices have grown to a crescendo, with even cardinals asking for married priests, including Cardinals Arns and Lorscheider of Brazil, Cardinal Pellegrino of Italy, Cardinal Hume of Britain, and Cardinal Darmojuwomo of Indonesia.[15] As long ago as the 1971 Synod, Cardinal Suenens asked for married priests.[16] Archbishop Malula of Kinshasa, Zaire, president of the African bishops, says we must ordain married couples to take over the catechesis.[17]

Archbishop William Borders of Baltimore expects changes. "Obviously we're going to have to rethink the approach we have to ordination," he said in August 1984, "because you know celibacy has never been a real doctrine. It's a matter of discipline. And any discipline in the Church can be changed or it can be suspended. So doctrine is not changed at all. It is discipline and custom that is affected."[18]

Bishop Jacques Gaillot of Evreux in Normandy in the 1988 annual gathering of the French bishops in Lourdes, called publicly for the ordination of married men. He criticized attempts to secure the return of priests from Lefebvre's extreme right-wing movement, while in the Church ordinary priests were being forced to leave because they wanted to marry, and good men were being refused ordination because they were not celibate.

"Is it not extraordinary that we deploy so much effort to bring back people who are far from Vatican II on essential points of faith," he asked, "while we are resigned to the departure of priests of value for the sole reason that they have rejected the undertaking of celibacy? How long are we going to deprive the ministry of married priests who remain available for service to the Church?"

In late 1988, the U.S. Bishops' Committee on Priestly Life and Ministry published a ground-breaking report that claimed a "serious and substantial morale problem" among the nation's priests, many of whom were overworked, lonely, and sexually troubled. For the first time speaking openly of problems long hidden, the bishops said some priests were just going through the motions, and many "have settled for a part-time presence to their priesthood." A major reason for these problems among the priests, and for clergy leaving the priesthood, was, according to the bishops, compulsory celibacy.[19]

These views are borne out in various interviews I have had with members of the Church's hierarchy.

"I personally believe," Cardinal Lorscheider told me in 1988, "that optional celibacy would be a stronger value—it would be a greater sign value, because many here [in Brazil] believe that a priest is only celibate because he is obliged to be. . . ."

Archbishop Flores of San Antonio, Texas, spoke to me of Protestant denominations in his area: "They have married clergy yet they are hard workers. Somehow marriage with them is not an obstacle. I could see the possibility [for us] of individuals who could be married and definitely effective."

Bishop Angelico Sandalo of São Paulo was emphatic on the

need for married priests. "I think this is a matter of urgency," he told me. "The more we work to try and have celibate priests, the less we have priests to attend all our people.

"To tie the exercise of priestly ministry to the charism of celibacy is merely a matter of discipline, and not in theology or early history. The Church ought to change it. Far more important than tying celibacy to the exercise of priesthood is that priests, married or not, should be present to the people."

Dom Angelico has put his finger on the nub of the issue (which is Schillebeeckx's second argument against compulsory celibacy): The whole controversy about priestly celibacy has now come down to as stark a choice as any in the history of the Church—we can have either compulsory celibacy *or* the mass. *We cannot have both.* There cannot be mass without an ordained minister, and as long as there is compulsory celibacy, there will not be enough ministers.

Dean R. Hoge, in his recent book *The Future of the Catholic Leadership,* states categorically that the key to vocations is that married men be ordained: "This option needs close examination because of its important effects. As we have seen, the celibacy requirement is the single most important deterrent to new vocations to the priesthood, and if it were removed the flow of men into seminaries would increase greatly, maybe fourfold. Therefore this option provides a solution to the shortage of priests."[20]

It is as simple as that. Hoge's conclusions are widely supported and underlined by overflowing U.S. Protestant seminaries, where enrollment rose from 42,627 in 1979 to 58,851 in 1983—an increase of 14.6 percent.

A study made by Catholic University makes it even clearer that rising opposition to celibacy is the key factor in the Catholic Church's decline in ministers. "There is no doubt," the study says, "that the celibacy requirement is a major hindrance to vocations today. Although it was not a major hindrance in past decades, social changes have produced new attitudes about sexuality, personal freedoms, and life-styles."

George Gallup, Jr., has concluded from surveys that about 5 percent of American youth are seeking some outlet for ministerial service, although they do not seek to be ordained.[21]

Gallup's and Hoge's conclusions are mirrored in other parts of the world. A paradox in Holland is that while the country's bishops and priests agonize about the future, there are over eight hundred young people, men and women, avidly studying theology at the country's universities. But they refuse point-blank to be ordained.[22]

In the third world too the number of priests is in drastic decline relative to the Catholic population, and we find African bishops calling for the ordination of local, married catechists. The problem is also reflected in Latin America. There the only possible source of native priests are the leaders to be found in local communities, who of course are married. They would, incidentally, be the best possible kind of priest, according to churchmen there—in touch with their people, already respected, already animators. Fr. George Protopapas writes, in another paper prepared for the Vatican Council: "In view of the present structure existing in South America and Central America, would it not be preferable and more advantageous for the Kingdom of God to have the priesthood conferred not only to celibates but also to married men? . . . The clergy must be able to count on as co-workers a married clergy. I mean by this that we should ordain as priests married men who have given proof of solid faith, good judgment, men who have given meaning to their life. At least quantitatively speaking the Church would be in a much better position to cope with the ever increasing population.[23]

It was in this context that Cardinal Hume's famous "call" for married priests took place. "At a meeting in Belgium," he told me, "we were discussing the situation in South America, where it was alleged that Christian communities were meeting around the word of God, and were not involving themselves in celebrating the Eucharist, because there were no priests. Well, my contribution was to say, 'I don't think it right and good that the Christian community should just live off scripture without the Eucharist. In such a situation, then, one might have to consider opening up the question of ordaining married men, so that people would not be deprived of the Eucharist and the Sacrament of Reconciliation.' It was some wretched reporter that turned it into headlines."

Hoge's book states categorically that the vocation shortage is long-term, not just temporary, and that it can be solved only through institutional measures. In a nutshell, then—if compulsory celibacy continues in the Catholic Church, there will be ever-increasing areas of the world that will be without priests, and therefore without the mass.

According to theologians, the People of God (that is, the

Church) have an absolute and inalienable right to the Eucharist. What, then, is to be said of those who would deprive them of that right by maintaining, in the face of all evidence, a compulsory celibacy?

So why is compulsory celibacy being maintained? One can only guess. The whole clerical ethos is bound up with it and could collapse if celibacy ended. As Cardinal Pallavicini, secretary of state to Pius VI, said around 1780, "If priests can marry, the papal hierarchy falls, the Pope loses respect and supremacy, married clergy will be tied by their wives and be dependent on the state."[24]

And compulsory celibacy is, or was, incredibly efficient—the ultimate management technique, giving total control and total mobility of personnel, and rendering priests independent of this-worldly interests and free of lay control.

Close to the kernel is the confusion between voluntary and compulsory celibacy, where arguments eminently valid for freely chosen celibacy are being misapplied to support a celibacy imposed by law on everyone.

Also today there is certainly an economic motive for retaining compulsory celibacy: If married priests and families enter the picture, Church authorities fear it would entail a drastic restructuring of Church finances. This fear has less basis than it would appear at first. Restructuring might be needed, but it would not necessarily cost more.

Inertia probably also has a great deal to do with Church reluctance to look again at celibacy: The Barque of Peter is rather like a supertanker, and takes a long time to slow up and set a new course.

Richard Schoenherr would see the Vatican's attitude as a last-ditch stand before radical change. As he put it to me in an interview: "It was Marx who said that no new form arises before a group is totally convinced that all the life is gone from the old form. How are we to know that life is gone from the compulsorily celibate male ministry, unless we extol it?"

He says it's a sort of last hurrah: "That explains the bizarre behavior, like not allowing girls to serve at the altar, yet allowing women to read the lessons. And like saying celibacy is a closed issue, and that there's no problem here, and that it's all the result of materialism.

"These are bizarre statements, flying in the face of reality. To

me it makes no sense, except sociologically: Before you bury something, you want to make sure it's dead. Rome is just beating a dead
horse, because they're not quite sure it's dead yet.''

Gianni Gennari in his *Paese Sera* column lays much at the door
of Pope John Paul II: ''Almost always the same problems, which he
continues to confront with his total refusal. The only reason for his
NO is the fact that he says NO, as if only he counted in the Catholic
Church. . . . And that NO counts against every possible YES,
against all the requests of everyone else, against all the recognized
pastoral needs, against all the positive findings of the worldwide
episcopate.''[25]

While little can be uttered in favor of enforcing celibacy on
all priests, in fairness it should be said that arguments are ad-
vanced against married priests that deserve to be looked at. Such
arguments can be summarized in three propositions: (1) a married
priest would be less available to God's people, less free for risks
or heroic actions; (2) he would be more tempted to a bourgeois
life-style; and (3) an uncommitted wife could impede his priestly
work.

Protestant pastor families could help us greatly in our study of
these questions. But let us not forget that already in the Catholic
Church we have a unique laboratory waiting to be worked—namely,
the priests who have already left and married, many of whom are
engaged in some kind of ministry.

In my encounters with these priest-families around the world,
I kept such questions in mind. And, without wishing to make Aunt
Sallies out of the questions (setting them up only to knock them
down), I am persuaded by what I have seen that they can all be
answered in favor of married priests. I can touch only briefly on
each here.

Availability? Undoubtedly a married priest will need time for
his family. One married priest, now back working full-time in a
West Coast parish (as a nonsacramental minister), asked his pastor
one day if he could come in late the following morning, as his wife
works and they had no baby-sitter.

''You have to be here,'' the pastor said.

''I can't tomorrow. You've got to understand I'm a married
person.''

''That's your problem.''

"Yes it is. And I'm taking the time my family needs," replied the married priest.

There are going to be many more interchanges like this if changes come to the celibacy law.

A married priest in Minnesota has been jailed a number of times for demonstrating against a corporation engaged in weapons research. This has been most difficult for his wife. "Sometimes," she told me, "I felt the kids and I are put on the back burner."

These are very real problems, but it does seem to be a matter of balance. It turned out that the priest with the baby-sitting problem was being required to work at the church from 7:00 A.M. until 10:30 every night. Of course there was a conflict. And the demonstrating priest now takes a lower profile and stays out of jail. Though he is less outwardly active, he told me, he is far more intensely involved in ecological and peace issues now, because he has children and their future to care about.

In Auschwitz, a celibate priest, Maximilian Kolbe, offered to take the place of the father of a family who was to be put to death. Today he is a saint. The Church will always have need for such heroes, but we have a far more immediate need for thousands more vocations, which compulsory celibacy is preventing.

According to Vilma Gozzini, an Italian theologian from Florence, Italy, the argument of greater availability as a justification for obligatory celibacy is not convincing. It is not availability, but the attitude in the heart of the minister that makes the difference, she says. And this attitude can be made positive and enriched by marital love and family.[26]

Fr. George Protopapas in his paper written for the bishops of Vatican II put the matter in a third world context:

> It is commonly said that celibacy permits a priest to belong to no one and to all. We are speaking here of the total [availability] which celibacy is supposed to guarantee. In an abstract setting this is true . . . but, according to the testimony of zealous and spiritual priests who work in these sectors, celibacy does not make them free, more at liberty to work, but, on the contrary, celibacy actually hinders their pastoral activities.
>
> This is paradoxical, but nonetheless true. In certain countries . . . the way of life of the celibate priest cate-

gorically prevents him from personally mingling with the
people and adjusting to the concrete reality, and consequently prevents him from assuming it and presenting it to
God. His celibacy confines him to the exercise of his
priesthood for himself and not for others. He lives separated from the stream of life, he becomes a priest for
himself and not for others. . . .The celibate priest cannot
take root among his people.[27]

Bourgeois life-style? In his book *A Theology of Liberation*,
Gustavo Gutierrez quotes in a footnote an open letter to Dutch
married priests from a group of Argentinian priests: "While you
were celibate, you did not know how . . . to be the voice of the
exploited countries, those suffering the consequences of the unjust
economic policy of the leaders of your countries. We hope that once
you are married you can do this better. Indeed, if marriage does not
help you to be more open to the world in general . . . you will have
accomplished nothing more than becoming more bourgeois. Remember that while you seek the right to establish a home, many
poor people in the Third World are renouncing theirs to give themselves completely to the liberation of their brother."[28]

A fair warning. I have met priests who married and who seem
to have sold out for a mess of pottage. Mercifully, I have not met
many, but they are a sad spectacle. However, the hundreds of other
married priests I have met convince me it does not have to be so.

I believe the key lies in continued dedication to the works of
mercy—"I was sick and you visited me; I was hungry and you gave
me to eat"—within the limits of one's situation. Members of a
married priest group that I met with in Colombia suggested it is all
about renouncing materialism: "The priests you meet, theoretically
celibate, are they less bourgeois, and more courageous? The situation of being bourgeois, whether married or not, depends on a
person's involvement with the consumer society, rather than on
being married or not. Materialism, not marriage, is what matters."

I found my ideal in those married priests who have continued
to work for the truly poor in Latin America. They and their families
live by the barrios and *favelas,* and their families seem imbued with
purpose.

Curiously enough, even for them, the kids are the danger. A
married priest in Lima, Peru, explained it to me: "You get

married—it doesn't change a thing. But having kids does. Do you really want to send your kids to that school up there? You know what it's like. What about a car to take them there? And what about a telephone? What about hygiene? Or what about growing up with the wrong accent?''

Joe and Jacqui McCarthy have made their decision: They are bringing up their little two-year-old boy right there on the edge of a Recife slum. I asked Joe if he wasn't being unfair to the child.

"We've thought about that," Joe said. "But no matter what you do, you are imposing on the child. Either way, the child doesn't get a chance to choose. Besides, the type of neighborhood we are mixing in, we feel we are doing the child a big service by letting him grow up in this environment. The values here—he has a lot more to gain here than anywhere else.''

But what about his future?

"The biggest service we can give to him is the example of our dedication, and the ideals we are trying to put into practice. In Christian terms, in faith terms, what we can pass on to him is the type of life we are living, which we are trying to make relevant, significant, and important. We don't feel we can give him anything more valuable than that. He'll grow up in that atmosphere, and he'll reach the point of choosing anyway.

"The other option? We'd live a life centered on getting on, being important, climbing ladders. Then he'd grow up with those values. It's one or the other.''

Will Joe and Jacqui be able to put enough money by for the youngster's education?

"The whole thing in our life is our insecurity. We can't plan for very long. We can't afford to worry. Jacqui comes from a wealthy family, but my father was a factory worker who never earned a lot and never worried about it. He passed on his values to me.'' They were giving themselves to God's service, Joe said. And they were trusting that God would provide.

I believe that people like Joe and Jacqui are truly prophetic— pioneers testing out paths for the very first time, paths that will be trodden by countless priest-families in the centuries to come.

The ideal must be a consummate balancing act: to live and bring up your children among the wretched of the earth, yet, rather than sink to becoming wretched too, to bring the wretched up to the standards, spiritual and material, you try to hold on to. And learning from those wretched, and trying to acquire their courage, their endurance, their sheer downright goodness. May God give you strength, Jacqui and Joe McCarthy. And your little boy too.

Uncommitted wives? Protestant denominations have long experience of varying levels of commitment on the part of a spouse—the spouse dedicated to ministry, verily the pastor's other half; the spouse who manages to balance being a minister's wife with a full life of her own; and the unconcerned spouse who resolutely goes her own way. Protestants manage to accommodate them all. And it's not confined to ministers: Tom Wolfe in his book *The Right Stuff* highlights the problems of being a wife to a dedicated aviator or astronaut.[29] Their problems appear tougher than those of any pastor's wife. Yet no one so far suggests celibacy for astronauts.

Marriages between nuns and priests appear to be more than usually successful. The reason often given is that a nun already shares much of the Church background and interests of her husband, as well as his pastoral drive. Much can be taken as understood, and she can relate more easily to his anguish and his fulfillment, as he can to hers. Such marriages are ideally suited to ministry. Either both partners could be involved in ministry, or at least the spouse would have an understanding and tolerance of the stresses of such work. I have seen examples of couples happily engaged in ministry, like Matt and Sandra Purcell. It is worth noting that 60 percent of the priests who marry in the United States take nuns as wives.

Also, one must distinguish between ordaining married men and inviting back to ministry those priests who had left to marry. The wives in each category are in quite different situations. If a married man were to be ordained, his wife presumably would be a party to that decision and be aware of the problems to be encountered. Whereas a woman who married a priest might not be at all agreeable to his returning to the ministry, and would have every right to say so. As Teresa, wife of the married priest Lauro Motta, told me in Fortaleza, Brazil, "To leave was his own decision. But to return to ministry would be *our* decision."

What it all amounts to is that making celibacy optional is no panacea. Of course it will bring new problems that will have to be faced.

There is an assumption that when the Church establishes a requirement, that requirement is seen to have a beneficial result for people. An excellent example is the requirement laid down for living in a monastery or in a religious order—namely, the vows of poverty, chastity, and obedience. For those who are suited to such a way of life (and relatively few are), the beneficial results are obvious. All of us have met the Thomas Mertons and the Mother Teresas of our local religious orders or missionary congregations, and they are an inspiration to us. In their case, the Church's requirements can be clearly seen as beneficial.

Can we say the same about the blanket celibacy requirement that is demanded of all secular priests living among us? Is it beneficial? In other words, does it promote growth and maturity, responsibility and spiritual development, in all or most of those priests? And is it beneficial to the community? It does none of those things. We have witnessed the havoc it causes to the souls and bodies of the individual priests who must endure compulsory celibacy, as well as to those associated with them. And we have witnessed the havoc it causes in the community, deprived of leaders and the mass.

We, the Church, the people of God, must come to a decision on compulsory celibacy, or lose the Eucharist that Jesus gave us. And if we make no decision? That, Dean Hoge points out, is a decision in itself. It is tantamount to opting for congregationalism—deciding for a Church without ordained ministers and without the mass.[30]

CHAPTER 12

Unless the Seed Die

So if you are offering your gift at the altar, and there remember that your brother has something against you, leave your gift there before the altar and go; first be reconciled to your brother, and then come and offer your gift.

Matthew 5:23–24

LEAVE your gift at the altar, and go first and be reconciled, says Jesus. It is so obvious, yet there are thousands of priests, celibate and married, who are not yet reconciled. All are growing older. Some are dying alienated from others. The laity and the new young priests are being handed this legacy of alienation of brother from brother. And the wives and the children of married priests are burdened with the same legacy: One hears wives sadly joking about children who come into this world "with more than original sin."

Yet how can a Church reconcile man to God, and preach reconciliation of man to man, when its own priests are still angry at one another? And what stops so many priests on either side from reaching out?

Fernando Iachini, a psychologist in Rome and a married priest who has known great anger, says we must first admit our anger, even our hatred. The priests who stayed must acknowledge their feelings against those they see as having betrayed them. Those who left must acknowledge their own sense of Church injustice: "At the bottom of our experience as priests who left is the consciousness that our Mother the Church did great violence to us as persons, depriving us of liberty, identity, maturity, individuality. That she was a *matrigna*—a stepmother—rather than a mother. This provoked our hatred toward the Church.

"But we had been taught in seminary never to hate, and this is impossible for man. We must first allow ourselves to hate what is human in the Church. God meets man where he is, on the sinful road. And hate is part of that.

"But then, we must overcome this hate with forgiveness. After hating, we must go one step further, and forgive. That is human maturity, and also Christian perfection."

Iachini says if we do not go beyond hate, if we do not get the courage to pardon the Church, we can never grow, never be at peace. And the same is true of priests who cannot pardon those who left. "We'll always be nailed to the cross of the past," he says.

Both resigned and active priests frequently expressed to me a longing for reconciliation. "The Church has undergone a terrible fragmentation," one resigned priest said to me. "I am one of those fragmented bits. I have a different community now—my family— but I am still very much aware of the religious community I left. Is there anyone who could take the leadership to see what connections can be made between us all?

"The Cross is in all our lives: I have the pain of departure; those who stayed have the pain of losing us, of reduced numbers, of reduced vocations. Could someone bring it all together—the love, the anger, the uncertainty, the fragmentation?

"I see myself still," he said, "as a part of the Dominican Order that formed me. I still think like them. I see myself almost as working out on a mission, trying to get by with whatever bit of spirituality I retain from my days in community.

"The founder of that order, early on, scattered his men all across the world. They still refer to it as the 'Scattering of the Seed.' Somehow I still feel as one of that scattered seed."

A psychologist and married priest, John Dubay, following fam-

ily therapy, suggests, in a letter, a three-part approach to reconciliation between priests.

First is to return, to go back to the source of the injury. As I
move toward the person, I gain strength to overcome feelings of
guilt, shame, and resentment. It restores some trust . . . and opens
the door to possible dialogue.

Second is dialogue. Here each side has to state needs and
expectations of the other side. As I ask something of you, I continue
to care enough about the relationship to risk your rejection and trust
you to be able to give to me.

Third is creating trust. We ask for consideration and try to give
it, making clear it is not an attempt to wipe the slate clean. Hope-
fully as we share the pains of our experience, new ways and options
to care for one another will be found.

Dubay points out that, just as marriage is not static, likewise
priesthood is something evolving and unfolding for each person.
Yves Congar had stressed that "the priesthood is essentially a prophetic rather than simply a ritual priesthood." If married priests
could be seen to have moved to new expressions of priesthood, then
there is really room for all. Dubay says: "Celibate priests would be
able to view married priests as resources and vice versa. Men who
once were brothers in grace could return to that state. . . . [It could
be a] resource to many celibates who are fighting great obstacles in
efforts to remain loyal to the Church. The journey of grace of the
married priest and his efforts to be loyal to his priesthood could be
the other side of the dialogue. A dialogue that could exonerate both
sides in their priestly existence and deepen their convictions.

"[The dialogue would reveal] a continuum of priestly existence. A sense of this continuum will make it possible in time to set
up rites of passage from one stage of priesthood to another. In time,
people will perhaps be called to ordination at various points on the
continuum. Rites of passage would also eliminate the pain that is
experienced now as one passes from the celibate to the married
priesthood . . . a transition which in the past has been seen as a
death would be seen in terms of life and growth."

There are, of course, many priests, both those who stayed
and those who left, who are already attaining personal reconciliation. When Fr. Joe Kramis gets a phone call from another Seattle
priest saying, "I've got three married priests in my parish. Will
you tell me how I can use them?"—it's a sign of redemption.

When the married priest Ron Titus can say, "I realize I had more or less excommunicated the pope. Well, now I accept him," it's redemption. As it is when Mark Zwick can say, "Somewhere along the line, Louise and I decided not to see the Church as an enemy. After the faith crisis of the sixties, the more we looked around, the more we came home again. We found we could live with the Church."

Reconciliation seems to come hardest to the institution itself. And the closer to the top of the pyramid, the less reconciliation there seems to be. So that we find the Vatican forbidding employment of married priests, withholding dispensations from men long married, sometimes until their deathbed, and failing in the simple courtesy of even acknowledging receipt of the petitions for dispensation. And we hear of the pope saying, "I'm in no hurry. We didn't leave them; they left us." I suppose it is understandable: The institution perceives the married priest as a threat to its structures. But it is sad, and so different from the father of the Prodigal Son who came running to meet him.

Yet further down the pyramid there are some splendid attempts at institutional reconciliation. The institution is only an abstraction, and these are men of flesh and blood who are reaching out. So we find Cardinal Bernardin of Chicago arranging pensions for all resigned priests who have given twenty years' service ("our brother, Joseph," some of the resigned priests call him).[1] There is a similar pension scheme in the diocese of Duluth, and a particularly generous one in Lafayette, Louisiana.[2]

Some of the religious orders, especially the missionaries, have evolved and matured considerably in their relationship to their married priests and families. Outstanding are Maryknoll, the Kiltegan Missionaries, and the Oblates. The Oblates, at their 1986 general chapter in Rome, formally declared their intentions toward their married priests: "In our apostolic ministry, we should willingly involve those former Oblates and laicized priests who might be disposed to serve the Church in collaboration with us—to the extent that Church law permits."[3]

My favorite story is from Holland. Every morning when the brethren of a famous monastery file to the chapel for mass and prayer, with them are a husband and wife in their sixties. Father Maarten had once been a priest of that community until he left twenty years ago and eventually married. He is now retired and has rejoined the community, this time with his wife. They have a small apartment on one of the floors of the monastery.

"He and his wife are well accepted there," a Dutch priest tells me. "She is a former religious sister. Both she and her husband perform a big role in the life of that community. They also organize series of lectures, and both of them preach at public masses."

It has been usual to think of the one hundred thousand priests who resigned formal ministry as "lost to the Church." However, one could see them as having simply moved to another part of the Church—moved from out of the clerical enclosure and in among the people of God. This is the first time that thousands of priests are meeting people without any barriers, sharing their joys and sorrows, hopes and fears, working with them, living family life among them, identifying with them. And above all, giving witness.

People watch. Once a man is known to be a resigned priest (and I believe it is both healthy and exhilarating to identify one's background), he is in a unique position to preach by example what he used to put in words. And to reach where a cleric could never go. With the added witness that he no longer "has to" live a life of dedication.

People do watch. If they can say about married priests and their families, "See how these Christians love one another," then the priest and his family become a leaven, transforming society from within, rather than preaching at it from outside. "A spiritual vortex" is what Fr. F. X. Murphy calls these priest-families—all told, a quarter of a million people, some of whom are quietly transforming both the world and the Church, just by the manner of their lives. Everywhere, they are bringing Christ into the workplace, simply by retaining Christian attitudes.

Archbishop Weakland of Milwaukee, Wisconsin, observed in 1986 how American Catholics have never really made the leap from personal spirituality to social action.[4] And priests are no more trained than laypeople to make that leap. Yet a priest at least has an education that could be the basis of awareness, and one who has already made that most drastic leap into lay life and marriage might make other leaps as well. If he can grow to hunger and thirst after justice (for others, not just for himself), and to act on it where possible, then he brings Christian values where there may have been few.

And there is no doubt whatsoever that the lives of good married priests and their families must in the long run transform the Church itself. For the Church, too, is watching. As Robert O'Brien has written:

> The Church is looking for signs of progress or regression in the spiritual vitality of married priests and of those influenced by this new state of Christian life. The process of discernment seeks to discover the "will of God," to look at evidence which is consistent with all that Christians believe about God. . . .
>
> The pioneers in living the priestly vocation and the calling to marriage are presenting God with evidence of a relative success or failure to grow in marital, parental, and community love. To the extent the married priests are patient, affectionate, caring and daring Christians, they are persuading God to foster their experiment. They are giving God evidence that strong love for God comes from married priests and their wives.
>
> The result will be a change in church policy. The change will be attributed to a synod, or to the Bishop of Rome, or to a papal congregation. But the discerning Catholic will know that the change is the will of God, consequent to the actions of the first generation of married Latin Rite priests and their spouses.[5]

It may take a long time. As the Chinese proverb goes, "The seed does not see the flower." But the Catholics of the next century must surely benefit from the lives of that first prophetic generation of married priests.

What in fact does the future hold for us, the Church? Here angels fear to tread. But certainly there are two distinct currents within the Church. I am reminded of the line from a poem, "Those behind cried forward, and those in front cried back."

First there is what can only be called a reactionary backlash, right at the very top of the pyramid. It is particularly obvious in a macabre race against death, wherein the present pope is appointing as many ultraconservative bishops as possible before his time runs out. It is a bit like a U.S. president packing the Supreme Court to ensure a continuation of his attitudes for decades to come.

Brazil, a great crucible of the Church, is cooling and darkening. "A shadow," says Penny Lernoux, "has begun to envelop Latin America's church of the poor. Slowly but inexorably, the institutional church is shifting away from a prophetic stance, to . . . political conservatism, through the continuing appointment of Vatican yes-men as bishops."[6] Whereas a champion of the poor, like Bishop Pedro Casaldaliga, is summoned to Rome for secret interrogation and told to sign a document admitting wrongdoing.[7]

Peru, the mother of liberation theology, has shifted emphatically to the right. Its hierarchy, once the most progressive in Latin America, is now packed with new bishops, described by Jesuit Jeffrey Klaiber as "timid, closed, and very dependent on the pope. They show little creativity or pastoral vision: they can only foster a weak and mediocre church."[8] In Chile, between 1977 and 1987, the Vatican replaced 12 of the country's 31 bishops with right-wing churchmen.[9] The pope is fashioning the United States, too, in his own image, having appointed almost 140 of the nation's bishops— almost half of those active. Similar things are happening in Holland, Austria, Germany, and Italy—the lights are going out all over Europe.[10]

All but one of Holland's former church leaders are gone, with ultraright-wingers now in six out of the seven dioceses. Holland, once a ferment of experimentation and hope, is sullenly turned off. "The Roman army of occupation," some Dutch priests are calling their new hierarchy.[11]

In 1988 the Church in Cologne, Germany, saw over three thousand people quit when ultraconservative Cardinal Joachim Meisner was forced on the diocese, against the will of the diocese and of the civil government and in violation of the spirit of the Concordat.[12]

Yet while these ultraconservative waves thunder on the beach, there is an undertow pulling powerfully toward change. It is a change more drastic than anything up to now. A radically altered world and Church have upped the ante, and the marriage of priests is now only one among many issues.

According to Rosemary Reuther, writing in the journal *America*, the Church is facing challenges, both within and without, in three separate areas. How it responds to these challenges will determine whether it can renew itself effectively and give witness and leadership in the world. There is the challenge from liberalism, democratic values, and human rights in the Church; the challenge from feminism and sexual morality; and the challenge from third world liberation. The future of priesthood and ministry is woven through all three.

In our day the Church has come around to speaking up for religious liberty, freedom of conscience, women's suffrage, democratic government, and human rights. And the world is willing to listen to Rome. As Reuther points out, the pope is probably the only global leader who would be listened to in all three worlds—capitalist, socialist, and third.

The challenge, however, is for Rome to practice what it preaches. And as yet, it fails to do so. Reuther says, "The partial rapprochement of the Catholic Church with liberal values is contradicted most blatantly by the inability of the Catholic hierarchy to apply these principles to itself as an institution. . . . In many . . . areas, such as fair wages, just contracts, the right of Church employees to unionize, the right of assembly and free press, the Catholic Church fails to apply to itself the civil rights it has defended in society."

The second challenge comes from feminism. The institutional Church is steeped in fear of sexuality and the fear of women. That is why it is kinder to clerics who use women than to clerics who marry them. We have dealt with the institution's fight to retain an unworkable celibacy, but the problem is now vastly broader and has to do with the institution's attempt to marginalize women completely. The question of whether priests can marry women is only a small part of the challenge: It has moved far beyond that to questions of whether women can adequately represent Christ and thus be ordained; of whether this male-run institution can continue to prohibit contraception, a prohibition that was maintained only so that the institution might not lose credibility by being seen to change.

And the third challenge, perhaps the greatest of all, comes from the fact that Catholicism is becoming more and more a third world Church. The challenge, then, is to move away from the rich and powerful and truly identify with the poor as they struggle to liberate themselves from unjust social structures that are contrary to the Gospel. It is the most daunting challenge of all, because, says

Reuther, "to defend the rights of the poor is to make oneself the marked target of those in power. . . . To opt for the poor is to lose one's place among the powerful, to choose vulnerability, perhaps torture and death. It is to choose to be a martyr church." It is the challenge of liberation theology.[13]

Questions of why priests leave, and whether celibacy should be optional, seem to grow pale and even self-indulgent when placed beside such massive challenges. Yet that is an illusion. Such questions are tightly interwoven in all three of those challenges. They are in fact a part of them. They are part of the struggle within the Church for human rights—the right to honorable dispensation, the right to marry, the right to have a family, the right to liberty under God. They are part of the feminist struggle, to which the institution is saying, you cannot be a priest if you are a woman or if you are married to one. And those questions are deeply a part of the option for the poor, because in the third world the only way those poor will have leadership or the Eucharist is if respected married family men can be drawn from within the community, and ordained to provide them with these two necessities.

The crisis in the priesthood is far from being a side issue. It is close to the center, jostled of course and sharing place with all these other issues—the full integration of women in the Church, including their ordination to the priesthood; the question of whether ministers should be drawn from their local community, and called by that community to serve, instead of being sent in from outside; even whether such ministers would derive their power from that community; the question of whether the ministry should be less sacral (Fr. Leonardo Boff describes it now as "a spiritual supermarket to which the priest holds the key") and more given to preaching the word of God; whether priestly ministry could be for a limited number of years; whether bishops and other leaders should hold office for a set period, as leaders of religious orders do.

The Rock of Peter is rocking, and already the stone floor of the Catholic Church has shifted under our feet. The Jesuit Fr. John A. Coleman explains there are several major ways in which this shift has occurred, none of which are likely to be reversed.[14]

There is the crisis of identity in male celibate priests, reflected in the vast exodus but even more in the worldwide refusal of sufficient Catholic men to become priests. Consequently, there is an ever-dwindling number of priests throughout the world.

Which leads to the most dramatic shift of all: The laity are moving in to take over. In answer to the worldwide scarcity of priests, there has been an explosion of nonordained ministries. In many parts of the third world, laypeople are appointed to do baptisms, marriages, eucharistic services, visitation and communion of the sick, burial services, preaching, counseling, parish administration—practically everything a priest used to do except the words of consecration and of absolution.

The laity, of course, are only taking back all the functions that were stolen from them by the clerics, functions only being yielded up because there are no longer enough clerics to do them. As Coleman points out, "It is in the interest of the Church, worldwide, to conceive of ministry in ways that undercut clerical caste, a sacred all-embracing order of ministry and mandates, by substituting instead the designations of natural leaders of a community for ministerial functions in the community."

So already, whether we like it or not, we are at the point where communities are selecting and putting forward their own ministers. And the laity are never going to give back what they have won. We are talking about the death knell of clericalism.

Also, like it or not, we already have married priests. Granted that so far only married convert Protestant clergy are being ordained priests, and granted Rome may have done it only for political reasons (it has been alleged that these clergy are welcomed precisely because they are generally opposed to women's ordination). However, the principle of an all-celibate clergy in the Roman Catholic Church has been breached. (It would be more accurate to say there never really was the principle of an all-celibate clergy, since, in the vast eastern part of the Catholic Church, priests have always been free to marry. Compulsory celibacy would be better viewed as a peculiarity of the western Latin rite of the Catholic Church, at odds with the more general principle of a married clergy throughout the Church.)

And we already have women pastors in the Catholic Church. Even in the United States, parishes are being handed over to nuns to run. One of a dwindling number of circuit-rider priests gallops in from time to time to preside at mass and consecrate some Hosts, and that's about it. Apart from that, Sister is Pastor, whether or not they give her that title. Is it any wonder, then, that people are asking why she is not ordained, especially when there is hardly a theologian of distinction today who objects on theological grounds to women's ordination?

"Make no misjudgment," Eugene Kennedy says. "Working out the conflict over an expanding role for women is the main business and moral obligation of the American Church in the next decade."[15] And not just the American Church: Women form half the people of God wherever they are found.

All these things are coming to pass, quietly, not in the administrative central bunker of the Catholic Church, but on the outer edges, and seeping inward toward the middle. There is nothing that can stop it.

What is really happening is that European Christianity is mutating into World Christianity, as Karl Rahner pointed out before his death.[16] This book is about a shattering—but it is really the Shattering of the old, European, Roman, clerical mold, which can no longer contain a Christianity of the World. And all the Roman appointments of reactionary bishops in the world can do no more for that mold than all the king's men were able to do for Humpty Dumpty.

Meanwhile there is ministry, full measure and overflowing, waiting to be done—enough for all the resigned priests in the world, and for all the lay ministers, and for all the women of the people of God.

And many of the priests who have left are no longer waiting for a nod from anyone: There is ministry to be done, and they are glad to take it upon themselves. They had never wanted to abandon ministry, except the formal clerical kind, just as they never wanted to abandon the Church. These are the men of whom Peter Hebblethwaite speaks: "They not only remain in the Church out of conviction, but they cannot conceive of leaving it, and for a very simple reason: They think of the Church simply as humanity, insofar as it has recognized, however falteringly, its vocation in Christ. They can no more leave the Church than they can take leave of humanity. To do so would be a form of spiritual suicide."

Priests who resign or who marry have not really left anything except the clerical condition. And there remains to all of them that most fundamental of all ministries, to do the ordinary things extraordinarily well, as St. Theresa said.

In November 1987, Cardinal Bernardin joined a group of married and resigned priests and their wives in Chicago to make a retreat together. In his homily at the close of the retreat, the cardinal said that an unremitting search for God's will is a key part of the role of resigned priests today:

> Sometimes the call to priesthood or religious life and the charism of celibacy no longer seem as simultaneous and inevitable as once they did, and you find yourself a resigned priest or a former religious trying to fit into a Church in desperate need of ministers. . . .
>
> As I listen prayerfully to today's Scripture readings, this is what I hear: that the Kingdom comes when people struggle to be faithful to Wisdom in the midst of sometimes unforeseen circumstances. . . . We can never give up, abandon the vigil, or assume that—for whatever reason—the issues we struggle with cannot somehow, someday, be worked out. To do so would be a breach of faith. For nothing happens without God's knowledge; nothing happens without some purpose.
>
> And this is the heart of what I want to say to you: let's not give up on one another, the Church, or the belief that—within this struggle, within this vigil for Wisdom— we shall find Wisdom sitting by our gate. . . .
>
> I will promise that I will struggle with you to discern where the Spirit is leading us. As with so many other complex, sensitive issues, I do not know the answers. But I do know that if we do not work together, if we do not keep watch together, our answers will be stillborn. . . .
>
> When people struggle to be faithful to Wisdom in the vagaries of life, the kingdom of God is made manifest. I have no facile solutions today, my sisters and brothers— only the deep belief and trust that our vigil in the night of this ambiguity will meet God's transforming Wisdom.
>
> I promise to watch and struggle with you.

That indeed is the prognosis for resigned and married priests— a future of struggle. It is, however, a struggle not against the Church, but hand in hand with all its priests and people, a struggle to find God's will, and waged in love. In the evening of your life, as Paul Claudel said, you will be judged on your love.

When I knelt all those many years ago to make my vows, my

Dominican superior held my hand and heard my heartfelt words. Then he solemnly said, *"Deus qui incepit, ipse perficiet"* ("God, who began this, will also bring it to perfection"). I believe those words will be fulfilled in the Holy Roman Catholic and Apostolic Church. I believe they will be fulfilled, too, in the struggle of every one of her priests—both those who remain clerics, and those who do not. For thou art a priest forever.

NOTES

Unofficial translations by the author from non-English originals are indicated by the word "translated." The word "author" in the notes refers to the author of this book.

PROLOGUE

1. *Il Resto del Carlino,* February 20, 1985. Translated.
2. Corpus: Fact Sheet on Crisis Caused by Priest Shortage. Minneapolis, 1987.
3. *Le Soir* (Brussels), August 31, 1987. Translated.
4. *MOMM* (Movement for the Ordination of Married Men) *Information Bulletin* 5 (December 1984): p. 26.
5. Corpus: Fact Sheet.
6. Pope John Paul II, address delivered in Philadelphia, October 1979.

CHAPTER 1

1. John L. McKenzie, S.J., *Authority in the Church* (London: Chapman, 1966), p. 183.
2. Jim Brandes did in fact briefly accept his assignment to Victoria, Texas, but left the ministry from there.
3. Letter, September 16, 1968, addressed to Pope Paul VI; Carlo Cardinal Confelonieri, prefect of Sacred Congregation of Bishops; Archbishop John F. Dearden, president, National Conference of Catholic Bishops; Archbishop Luigi Raimondi, apostolic delegate to the United States; Archbishop Robert E. Lucey of San Antonio, Texas. Signed by fifty-one priests in the Archdiocese of San Antonio. A further seventeen signatures were added later. Photocopy in author's files.
4. *Diocesan Directory,* San Antonio, Texas, 1967 and 1988 editions.

5. Richard Schoenherr, "Trends in Ministry: Patterns in Decline and Growth," lecture.

6. Corpus: Fact Sheet, 1987.

7. Information from Professor Richard Schoenherr, Sociology Department, University of Wisconsin at Madison.

8. Corpus: Fact Sheet, 1987.

9. *Corpus Reports* 11, no. 6 (November 1985): 1.

10. Corpus: Fact Sheet, 1987.

11. Information from Professor Richard Schoenherr, Sociology Department, University of Wisconsin at Madison.

12. *Figaro* (Paris), November 3, 1987, "Notre Vie" sect. Translated.

13. Ibid.

14. Information from Gianni Gennari, Rome.

15. KASKI report. Den Haag, Holland, 1983. Updated by Fr. Lambert van Gelder.

16. Irish Catholic Bishops' Council for Research & Development. Figures up to 1985 only. Supplied to author by council office in Maynooth, Ireland.

17. Information from Rumos, Brasilia.

18. Information from Fr. Michael Gaine, professor of sociology at Christ's and Notre Dame College, Liverpool.

19. *Annuarium Statisticum Ecclesiae.* Vatican City. Quoted in *Corpus Reports* 12, no. 5 (September-October 1986).

20. Corpus: Fact Sheet, 1987.

21. Lucas Grollenberg et al., *Minister? Pastor? Prophet?* (London: SCM Press, 1980), p. 10.

22. John A. Coleman, S.J., "The Future of Ministry," *America,* no. 144, March 28, 1981, p. 248; also *Clergy Review* 62 (London) (1977): 26–32.

23. *Le Soir* (Brussels), August 31, 1987. Translated.

24. Coleman, "The Future of Ministry," p. 247.

CHAPTER 2

1. Penny Lernoux, paper delivered at 2nd Inter-American Meeting of Catholic Religious at Bogota, Colombia, August 1974. Quoted in Penny Lernoux, *Cry of the People* (London: Penguin, 1982), p. 454.

2. Mario Pancera, *I Novi Preti* (Milan: Sperlinge-Kupfer, 1977), pp. 145–69. Translated.

3. Canon 284 of the 1983 Code of Canon Law requires clerics to wear "suitable ecclesiastical dress" in accordance with the norms established by the episcopal conference or by legitimate local custom.

4. *Commonweal,* October 13, 1978, pp. 655–58.

CHAPTER 3

1. Elisabeth Kübler-Ross, *On Death and Dying* (New York: Macmillan, 1977), pp. 110ff.
2. *Time,* February 23, 1970, pp. 54–55.
3. Antonio Corsello, *È Tempo di Parlare* (Rome: Seristampa Comiso, 1986), p. 69. Translated.
4. Ibid., p. 61.
5. Ibid., p. 58.
6. Ibid., p. 62.
7. *The Wall Street Journal,* April 24, 1979, p. 1.
8. *National Catholic Reporter,* January 29, 1982.

CHAPTER 4

1. *Western People,* December 16, 1981, p. 15.
2. *Paese Sera,* January 20, 1983. Translated.
3. Ibid.
4. Benedict Williamson, *The Treaty of the Lateran* (London: Burns, Oates & Washbourne, 1929), p. 54.
5. Mario Pancera, *I Novi Preti* (Milan: Sperlinge-Kupfer, 1977), pp. 11–36. Translated.
6. Williamson, *Treaty,* p. 62.
7. Information from Fr. Lambert van Gelder, Nijmegen, Holland, who reports that the matter was widely featured in the Dutch press.
8. Information from Professor Eduardo Hoornaert, Fortaleza, Brazil.
9. *Charisma,* November 1983, p. 22.
10. Photocopy of letter in author's files.
11. Paul Winninger, "Powers & Duties of Holy Orders," p. 10 (unpublished document prepared in advance for those taking part in the Second Vatican Council and marked "Secret"). Copy in author's files.
12. Copy of letter in author's files.
13. Photocopy of letter in author's files. Translated.
14. *Paese Sera,* December 22, 1984. Translated.
15. *Rumos,* May-June 1987, p. 4.
16. Telephone interview with author.
17. Reported to author by three different U.S. priests, none of whom wished to be identified.
18. Reported to author, August 1987, by Luciano Paglialunga, the Italian married priest to whom it happened.
19. Questionnaire for Petitioners for Laicization with a Dispensation from All Obligations Arising from Solemn Profession and Sacred Ordination. Copy in author's files.

20. *Concilium No. 73* (New York: Herder, 1972), pp. 107ff.

21. Congregation for the Doctrine of the Faith: Private Instruction to Ordinary. Vatican City: March 7, 1975. Photocopy in author's files.

22. James A. Coriden, Thomas J. Green, and Donald E. Heintschel, *The Code of Canon Law: A Text & Commentary* (London: Geoffrey Chapman, 1985), pp. 236–37.

23. Van Dijk, B., and Salemink, Th., *Van Beroep: Pastor* (Hilversum, Netherlands: Gooi & Sticht, 1986).

CHAPTER 5

1. Eugene C. Kennedy, and Victor J. Heckler, *The Catholic Priest in the United States: Psychological Investigations* (Washington, D.C.: United States Catholic Conference, 1972), p. 51.

2. Ibid., p. 12.

3. Eugene Kennedy et al., "Clinical Assessment of a Profession: Roman Catholic Clergyman," *Journal of Clinical Psychology* 33, no. 1 (January 1977).

4. Ibid.

5. Rollo May, *Love & Will* (New York: W. W. Norton & Co., 1969), p. 311.

CHAPTER 6

1. Report by Dr. Terence Dosh on Corpus survey, Minneapolis, 1987, p. 6.

2. *National Catholic Reporter,* March 25, 1988.

3. Edward Kelly, *Cry Out to the Church* (Quezon City, Philippines: Phoenix Publishing House, Inc., 1984), pp. 175–76.

4. Edward Schillebeeckx, *Ministry* (London: SCM Press, 1981), p. 77.

5. James A. Coriden, Thomas J. Green, and Donald E. Heintschel, *The Code of Canon Law: A Text & Commentary* (London: Geoffrey Chapman, 1985), can. 1752.

6. Listing compiled by Corpus, 1987.

CHAPTER 7

1. *Sojourners,* December 12, 1987, pp. 12–15. This very beautiful and moving article by Vicki Kemper and Larry Engel is the basis of the story.

2. *Seattle Times*, March 15, 1987, p. B1.

3. *The New York Times*, September 11, 1987. Report of *The New York Times*-CBS News poll conducted August 24 to September 1, 1987.

4. *Los Angeles Times*, August 20, 1986,

5. *Upturn*. Bulletin of Association of Chicago Priests. Tim O'Connell: "The Look of a Happy Priest." Photocopy of undated article.

6. Andrew M. Greeley, *The Cardinal Sins* (New York: Warner, 1981).

7. *Breviary of the Order of Preachers*, Eng. lang. ed. (Dublin: Dominican Publications, 1967). Pt. 1, p. 1109.

8. Paul I. Murphy, *La Popessa* (New York: Warner Books, 1983),

9. Guus Van Hemert, *Some Remarks on Teilhard de Chardin's L'Évolution de la Chastété* (offprint from *Fides Sacramenti: Sacramentum Fidei*) (Nijmegen, Netherlands: Van Gorcum, 1981).

CHAPTER 8

1. Anne Lueg, ed., *Ein Sprung in der Kette* (Solingen, Germany: Initiativgruppe der vom Zölibat betroffenen Frauen, 1985).

2. Ursula Goldmann-Posch, *Unheilige Ehen* (Munich: Kindler Verlag, GmbH, 1985).

3. *Katholische Nachrichten Agentur*, January 30, 1985. Translated.

4. Stephen Pfürtner, "Pathology of the Catholic Church," *Concilium* 73 (1972): 28.

5. *St. Anthony Messenger*, August 1986, Note: "Fr. William Wells" is a pseudonym.

6. *The Record*, August 8, 1986, p. A16.

7. *Catholic Herald* (London), May 8, 1987, p. 4.

8. *De Tijd*, August 7, 1981, pp. 36–41.

9. *Now Is the Time*. Bulletin of the Advent Group (London) (August 1986): 11. (Advent translation of letter that originally appeared in *Batir*, the bulletin of Marseilles married-priest group.)

10. Ibid., p. 11.

11. Document written by interviewee for this book and reproduced here with her written permission. Original in author's file.

12. From A. W. Richard Sipe, *The Search for Celibacy: Practice, Process, and Achievement* (New York: Brunner/Mazel, 1990). Used with permission.

13. Richard Sipe, address delivered June 17, 1988, to the First U.S. National Conference on a Married Priesthood, American University, Washington, D.C., June 17–19, 1988.

14. *Commonweal*, June 19, 1987, p. 382.

15. Heinz-Jürgen Vogels, *Sieb des Satans* (Bornheim, Germany: Franz Paffenholz, 1966).

16. "Clerical Celibacy: An Asset or a Liability?" p. 2 (unpublished document prepared in advance for those taking part in the Second Vatican Council and marked "Secret"). No author's name. Copy in this author's files.

17. Augustus Y. Napier and Carl A. Whitaker, *The Family Crucible* (New York: Harper & Row, 1978), pp. 20ff.

18. John A. O'Brien, ed., *Why Priests Leave* (New York: Award Books, 1970), p. 182.

CHAPTER 9

1. National Opinion Research Center, *The Catholic Priest in the United States: Sociological Investigations* (Washington, D.C.: United States Catholic Conference, 1972), pp. 281–82.

2. *MOMM* (Movement of the Ordination of Married Men) *Information Bulletin* 4 (April 1984): 49.

3. Yves Congar, O. P., *Communidades Ecclesiais de Base* (Petropolis, Brazil: Vozes, 1973), pp. 144–45.

4. Thomas Merton, "Thomas Merton e celibato," *Vozes* (July 1967). Translated.

5. *The Irish Times* (Dublin), December 29, 1988, p. 10.

6. Sanford M. Dornbusch, "The Military Academy as an Assimilating Institution," *Social Forces* 33, no. 4 (May 1955): 316–21. Abridged in Leonard Broom and Philip Selznick, *Sociology* (New York: Harper & Row, 1969), pp. 110–13.

7. A. W. Richard Sipe, address to National Guild of Catholic Psychiatrists, Montreal, Canada, May 8, 1988.

8. Richard A. Schoenherr, "Power and Authority in Organized Religion: Disaggregating the Phenomenological Core," *Sociological Analysis* 47 (1987): 54.

9. Max Weber, *The Sociology of Religion,* trans. Ephraim Fischoff (Boston: Beacon Press, 1963), p. 29.

10. Robert K. Merton, *Social Theory & Social Structure* (New York: Free Press, 1968), pp. 251–56.

11. H.A.L. Fisher, *A History of Europe* (London: Fontana, 1968), vol. 1, p. 418.

12. John P. Dolan, *History of the Reformation* (New York: Desclee Co., 1965), p. 231.

13. *The Tablet* (London), August 18, 1984, pp. 788–89.

14. *The New York Times,* October 22, 1986.

15. Information from Fr. Brian Holmes CSSR, Fortaleza, Brazil.

16. *National Catholic Reporter,* November 13, 1987.

17. Dolan, *History of the Reformation,* p. 227.

18. Hubert Jedin, "The Celibacy of Priests in the 16th Century," pp. 1–2 (unpublished document prepared in advance of the Second Vatican Council and marked "Secret"). Copy in author's files.

19. Priests for Equality pastoral, *Toward a Full and Equal Sharing* (West Hyattsville, Md.) December 8, 1985, art. 2, p. 1.

20. Ibid., art. 33, p. 20.

21. *AGEN Bulletin,* São Paulo, Brazil, January 16, 1988, pp. 2–3.

22. *The Tablet* (London), December 12, 1987, p. 1346, and Robert Blair Kaiser, *The Encyclical That Never Was: The Story of the Pontifical Commission on Population, Family and Birth, 1964–66* (London: Sheed & Ward, 1987).

23. Leonardo Boff, *Ecclesiogenesis* (New York: Orbis Books, 1986), p. 2.

24. Congar, *Communidades,* pp. 144–45.

25. *MOMM Information Bulletin* 9 (October 1988): 32. Text of lecture by Bishop P. Kalilombe at the annual general meeting of MOMM, March 10, 1988, in London.

26. "The Conflict Situation of the Priest in the Modern World" (unpublished document prepared in advance of the Second Vatican Council and unsigned).

CHAPTER 10

1. CO.SA.RE.SE. Bulletin, Barcelona-Madrid, March 1987, pp. 3, 41–42.

2. *Paese Sera,* June 23, 1986. Translated.

3. Universal Synod of Married Catholic Priests and Wives, report to the synod of the conversation of the secretary, Paolo Camellini, and the coordinators Lambert van Gelder and Heinz-Jürgen Vogels, with Msgr. Canciani, pastor in Rome and consultor of the Congregation of Clergy, Rome, February 25, 1985.

4. Both documents are unpublished; they were circulated as photocopied typescripts in advance of the International Congress of Married Priests and Wives at Ariccia, Italy, August 23–28, 1987.

CHAPTER 11

1. Eknath Easwaran, *Gandhi the Man* (Petaluma, Calif.: Nilgiri Press, 1983).

2. Charles A. Gallagher and Thomas L. Vandenberg, *The Celibacy Myth: Loving for Life* (New York: Crossroads Publishing Co., 1987).

3. *Corpus Reports* 12, no. 1 (January-February 1986): 2.

4. Edward Schillebeeckx, *The Church with a Human Face: A New & Expanded Theology of Ministry* (London: SCM Press, 1985), pp. 240–49.

5. Joan O'Hanneson, *And They Felt No Shame* (Minneapolis: Winston Press, 1983), p. 93.

6. John P. Dolan, *History of the Reformation* (New York: Desclee Co., 1965), p. 226.

7. O'Hanneson, *And They Felt No Shame,* p. 93.

8. Matilda Joslyn Gage, *Woman, Church & State* (Salem N.H.: Ayer Co., 1985), pp. 72–84.

9. Hubert Jedin, "The Celibacy of Priests in the 16th Century," pp. 1–2 (unpublished document prepared in advance of the Second Vatican Council and marked *"sub secreto"*).

10. Ibid., p. 1.

11. *Gaudium et Spes: Pastoral Constitution on the Church in the Modern World,* par. 49. One of sixteen official texts, promulgated by the Second Vatican Council, December 7, 1965. Published in Walter M. Abbott, S.J., ed., *The Documents of Vatican II* (London: Geoffrey Chapman, 1966), p. 253.

12. Schillebeeckx, *The Church with a Human Face,* p. 249.

13. Lucas Grollenberg et al., *Minister? Pastor? Prophet?* (London: SCM Press, 1980), p. 13.

14. Ibid.

15. Corpus: fact sheet, 1987.

16. *MOMM Information Bulletin* 6 (April 1985): 4.

17. *Now Is the Time,* Bulletin of the Advent Group (London), May 1988, p. 4.

18. *Corpus Reports* 11, no. 3 (May-June 1985): 2.

19. *Report of U.S. Bishops Committee on Priestly Life and Ministry.* Information from Associated Press report by David Briggs, published December 26, 1988.

20. Dean Hoge, *Future of Catholic Leadership* (Kansas City: Sheed & Ward, 1987), pp. 144–45.

21. Ibid., p. 190.

22. Information from Fr. Lambert van Gelder, Nijmegen, Netherlands.

23. George Protopapas, "The Priesthood & Celibacy in the Modern World," p. 2 (unpublished document prepared in advance of the Second Vatican Council and marked *"sub secreto"*).

24. *MOMM Information Bulletin* 8 (February 1987): 16.

25. *Paese Sera,* July 14, 1984.

26. Address delivered by Vilma Gozzini to the International Congress of Married Priests and Wives, Ariccia, Italy, August 23–28, 1987.

27. Protopapas, "The Priesthood & Celibacy," p. 2.

28. Gustavo Gutierrez, *A Theology of Liberation* (London: SCM Press, 1974), pp. 122–123.

29. Tom Wolfe, *The Right Stuff* (New York: Bantam, 1980), pp. 1–5, 13, 338–39.

30. Hoge, *Future of Catholic Leadership*, p. 214.

CHAPTER 12

1. Letter of Joseph Cardinal Bernardin mailed to the resigned priests of Chicago archdiocese, June 22, 1987. Photocopy in author's files.

2. Information from Dr. Terry Dosh.

3. Oblates of Mary Immaculate. Acts of General Chapter, 1986.

4. Archbishop Rembert Weakland, O.S.B., "The Church in Worldly Affairs," *America,* October 18, 1986, p. 202.

5. *Corpus Reports* 11, no. 4 (July-August 1985): 3.

6. *National Catholic Reporter,* 17 June 1988, p. 7.

7. Ibid., October 7, 1988, p. 1.

8. Ibid., June 17, 1988, p. 9.

9. Ibid.

10. Ibid., pp. 16–17.

11. Information from Evert Verheijden, president of GOP, the Netherlands.

12. *The Irish Times* (Dublin), January 11, 1989, p. 6.

13. Rosemary Ruether, "Crises and Challenges of Catholics Today," *America,* March 1, 1986, pp. 152–58.

14. John A. Coleman, S.J., "The Future of Ministry," *America,* no. 144, March 28, 1981, pp. 243–49.

15. Eugene Kennedy, *The Now and Future Church: The Psychology of Being an American Catholic* (Garden City, N.Y.: Doubleday, 1984), p. 177. As quoted in Dean Hoge, *Future of Catholic Leadership* (Kansas City: Sheed & Ward, 1987), p. 211.

16. John P. Glaser, "Epoch III: The Church Feminized," *Commonweal,* no. 44, January 28, 1983, pp. 44–45.

BIBLIOGRAPHY

THE following are the principal books and documents consulted. There were also 1,123 other smaller documents, such as letters, news reports, and articles.

Abbott, Walter M. *Documents of Vatican II*. London: Geoffrey Chapman, 1966.

Aceros Caceres, Hugo. *Vamos P'Alante*. Bogota: Barreto Gama, 1982.

Archdiocese of San Antonio. *Diocesan Directory*. San Antonio, Texas, 1967 and 1988 editions.

Baligand, Pierre et al. *Échanges et Dialogue: La Mort du Clerc*, Paris: Idoc, 1975.

Barfield, Charles G. "Of Murphy's Law and Woman." Private circulation, 1987.

Barrett, E. Boyd. *Shepherds in the Mist*. London: Burns Oates, 1951.

Bellah, Robert et al. *Habits of the Heart*. New York: Harper & Row, 1985.

Billanovich, Augusto. *Sacerdozio e Celibato*. Treviso: Longo & Zoppelli, 1925.

Bishops' Committee on Priestly Life and Ministry, ed. "A Shepherd's Care: Reflections on the Changing Role of Pastor." Washington, D.C.: U.S. Catholic Conference, 1987.

Boff, Leonardo. *Church: Charism & Power*. New York: Crossroads, 1985.

——. *Ecclesiogenesis*. New York: Orbis Books, 1986.

Bohan, Murray et al. *Being a Priest in Ireland Today*. Dublin: Dominican Publications, 1988.

Bossa, Benjamin. *O Direito de Amar: A Queda de um Tabu*. São Paulo: Bossa, 1984.

Breviary of the Order of Preachers. Eng. lang. ed. Dublin: Dominican Publications, 1967.

Bronder, Saul. *Social Justice and Church Authority: The Public Life of Archbishop Robert E. Lucey.* San Francisco: Temple University Press, 1982.

Broom, Leonard, and Philip Selznick. *Sociology.* New York: Harper & Row, 1969.

Carney, J. Guadalupe. *To Be a Revolutionary.* San Francisco: Harper & Row, 1985.

Carroll, Denis. *What Is Liberation Theology?* Cork: Mercier Press, n.d.

CEF Secretariat. *Fidelité, Célibat et Ministère.* Paris: Conference Episcopale Française, 1976.

"Clerical Celibacy: An Asset or a Liability?" Unpublished document prepared for those taking part in the Second Vatican Council, 1963.

Communità di San Paolo. *Il Cristiano e la Sessualità.* Rome: Com-Nuovi Tempi, 1980.

"The Conflict Situation of the Priest in the Modern World." Unpublished document prepared for those taking part in the Second Vatican Council, 1963.

Congar, Yves. *Power & Poverty in the Church.* London: Chapman, 1964.

Congregation for the Doctrine of the Faith. Vatican City: Private Instruction to Ordinary, 1975.

Connetable, Jean et al. *Mariés, mais Toujours Prêtres?* Brussels: CEFA, c. 1980.

Cooney, John. *No News Is Bad News: Communications Policy in the Catholic Church.* Dublin: Veritas, 1974.

Coriden, James A., Thomas A. Green, and Donald E. Heintschel. *The Code of Canon Law: A Text and Commentary.* London: Geoffrey Chapman, 1985.

Corsello, Antonio. *È Tempo di Parlare.* Rome: Seristampo Comiso, 1986.

———. *Una Chiesa e un Ambiente che Opprimono.* Rome: Privitera, 1970.

Crow, Richard. "Second Journeys: A Study of Married Priests and Their Wives." Master's thesis, Fielding Institute, 1978.

De Broucker, Jose. *Dom Helder Camara.* London: Collins, 1977.

De Rosa, Peter. *Vicars of Christ.* New York: Crown Publishers, 1988.

Dolan, John P. *History of the Reformation.* New York: Desclée & Co., 1965.

Donahue, John M., and David B. Oliver. *Attrition & the Future of the Catholic Foreign Mission Society of America.* San Antonio: Trinity University, 1976.

Easwaran, Eknath. *Gandhi the Man.* Petaluma, Calif.: Nilgiri Press, 1983.

Ebaugh, Helen. *Out of the Cloister.* Austin: University of Texas Press, 1977.

Egan, John P., and Paul D. Colford. *Baptism of Resistance, Blood, and Celebration.* Mystic, Conn.: Twenty-Third Publications, 1983.

Fisher, H.A.L. *A History of Europe.* London: Fontana, 1968.

Franzoni, Giovanni. *Tra la Gente.* Rome: Com-Nuovi Tempi, 1976.

Gage, Matilda Joslyn. *Woman, Church, and State.* Salem, N.H.: Ayer Co., 1985 (reprint of 1893 edition).

Gallagher, Charles A., and Thomas L. Vandenburg. *The Celibacy Myth: Loving for Life.* New York: Crossroads, 1987.

Goergen, Donald. *The Sexual Celibate.* London: SPCK, 1979.

Goldman-Posch, Ursula. *Unheilige Ehen.* Munich: Kindler Verlag GmbH, 1985.

Graham, William L. "The Psychological Experiences of Resigned Roman Catholic Priests." Ph.D. dissertation, Union Graduate School, 1985.

Greeley, Andrew M. *The Cardinal Sins.* New York: Warner, 1981.

———, and Mary Greeley Durkin. *How to Save the Catholic Church.* New York: Viking, 1984.

Grollenberg, Lucas et al. *Minister? Pastor? Prophet?* London: SCM Press, 1980.

Gutierrez, Gustavo. *A Theology of Liberation.* London: SCM Press, 1974.

Haag, John E. "A Study of the Seminary and Priesthood Experience of Thirteen Resigned Roman Catholic Priests." Ph.D. dissertation, Pittsburgh Theological Seminary, 1984.

Hamburger, Gerd. *La Fine di un Tabù: Il Matrimoni dei Preti.* Turin: Piero Gribaudi, 1969 (from German original).

Hebblethwaite, Peter. *In the Vatican*. Oxford: Oxford University Press, 1987.

Hegarty, Martin J. *Woerc Directory*. Chicago: Woerc, 1986.

Hendricks-Rauch, Maureen. "A Study of the Marriages and Marital Adjustment of Resigned Roman Catholic Priests and their Wives." Ph.D. dissertation, University of Colorado, 1979.

Hoge, Dean. *Future of Catholic Leadership*. Kansas City: Sheed & Ward, 1987.

Jacobelli, M. Caterina. *Sacerdozio, Donna, Celibato*. Rome: Borla, 1981.

Jedin, Hubert. "The Celibacy of Priests in the 16th Century." Unpublished document prepared for those taking part in the Second Vatican Council, 1963.

Joannes, Fernando. *Padres Amanhã?* Petrópolis, Brazil: Vozes, 1970.

Kavanaugh, James. *The Celibates*. New York: Avon, 1985.

Kelly, Edward. *Cry Out to the Church*. Quezon City, Philippines: Phoenix Publishing House, Inc., 1984.

Kennedy, Eugene C., and Victor J. Heckler. *The Catholic Priest in the United States: Psychological Investigations*. Washington, D.C.: United States Catholic Conference, 1972.

Kenny, Anthony. *A Path from Rome*. Oxford: Oxford University Press, 1986.

Kübler-Ross, Elisabeth. *On Death and Dying*. New York: Macmillan, 1977.

Küng, Hans. *Why Priests?* London: Collins, 1972.

Lernoux, Penny. *Cry of the People*. London: Penguin, 1982.

Lueg, Anne, ed. *Ein Sprung in der Kette*. Solingen: Initiativgruppe der vom Zölibat betroffenen Frauen, 1985.

Lukas, Mary, and Ellen Lukas. *Teilhard*. New York: McGraw-Hill, 1981.

McKenzie, John L., S.J. *Authority in the Church*. London: Chapman, 1966.

McMurtrey, Martin. *The Mariachi Bishop: The Life Story of Patrick Flores*. San Antonio: Corona, 1987.

Merriman, Brian. *The Midnight Court*. Translated by Cosslett O. Cuinn. Cork: Mercier, 1987.

Merton, Robert K. *Social Theory & Social Structure*. New York: Free Press, 1968.

Miles, Michael. *Love Is Always*. New York: William Morrow, 1986.

Mocciaro, Rosario. *Dichíarazione d'Identità del Movimento "Vocatio."* Vocatio, Via Ostiense 152-B, Rome, Italy.

————, and Luigi Bettazzi. *La Communità dell'Abate Franzoni*. Rome: Napoleone, 1973.

Murphy, Paul I. *La Popessa*. New York: Warner, 1983.

Napier, Augustus Y., and Carl A. Whitaker. *The Family Crucible*. New York: Harper & Row, 1978.

National Opinion Research Center. *The Catholic Priest in the United States: Sociological Investigations*. Washington, D.C.: United States Catholic Conference, 1972.

North Country Curate. *Via Dolorosa*. London: Sands, n.d.

O'Brien, John A., ed. *Why Priests Leave*. New York: Award Books, 1970.

Occhiogrosso, Peter. *Once a Catholic*. Boston: Houghton Mifflin, 1987.

O'Hanneson, Joan. *And They Felt No Shame:* Minneapolis: Winston Press, 1983.

Padovano, Anthony. *Pastoral Ministry and the Non-Clerical Priesthood*. Minneapolis: Corpus Research, 1989.

Pancera, Mario. *I Novi Preti*. Milan: Sperlinge-Kupfer, 1977.

Podestà, Jeronimo, and Clelia Podestà. *Caminos de Libertad*. Buenos Aires: Planeta Argentina, 1985.

Potel, Julien. *Ils se sont Mariés . . . et Après?* Paris: L'Harmattan, 1986.

Potter-Seasons, Lisa. *No Weapon Save Love*. Hantsport, Nova Scotia: Lancelot, 1983.

Prefontaine, Marjorie. "Transition: A Study of the Process Experienced by Roman Catholic Ex-clerics." Ph.D. dissertation, Texas Woman's University, 1987.

Priests for Equality pastoral. "Toward a Full and Equal Sharing." West Hyattsville, Md.: Priests for Equality, 1985.

Protopapas, George. "The Priesthood & Celibacy in the Modern World."

Unpublished document prepared for those taking part in the Second Vatican Council, 1963.

St. Anthony, Neal. *Until All Are Housed in Dignity*. Minneapolis: Project for Pride in Living, 1987.

Schillebeeckx, Edward. *The Church with a Human Face: A New & Expanded Theology of Ministry*. London: SCM Press, 1985.

———. *Ministry*. London: SCM Press, 1981.

Schmitt, João Basílio, ed. *MPC Catalogo Geral*. Brasilia: Associacão Brasiliense de Padres Casados, 1984.

Sheppard, David, and Derek Worlock. *Better Together*. London: Hodder & Stoughton, 1987.

Thomas, Gordon. *Desire and Denial*. New York: Little, Brown, 1984.

Unesco. *Human Rights: Comments and Interpretations*. London: Allen Wingate, 1950.

Van Dijk, B., and Th. Salemink. *Van Beroep: Pastor*. Hiversum: Gooi & Sticht, 1986.

Van Hemert, Guus. *Some Remarks on Teilhard de Chardin's L'Évolution de la Chasteté* (offprint from *Fides Sacramenti: Sacramentum Fide*). Nijmegen, Netherlands: Van Gorcum, 1981.

Vogels, Heinz-Jürgen, *Pficht-Zölibat*. Munich: Kosel-Verlag, 1978.

———. *Sieb des Satans*. Bornheim: Franz Paffenholz, 1966.

Weber, Elizabeth, and Barry Wheaton. "The Career Change of Atlantic Area Roman Catholic Diocesan Priests after Vatican II." Ph.D. dissertation, Mount St. Vincent University, 1985.

Weber, Max. *The Sociology of Religion*. Translated by Ephraim Fischoff. Boston: Beacon Press, 1963.

Williamson, Benedict. *The Treaty of the Lateran*. London: Burns, Oates & Washbourne, 1929.

Winninger, Fr. Paul. "Powers and Duties of Holy Orders." Unpublished document prepared for those taking part in the Second Vatican Council, 1963.

Winter, Michael. *Whatever Happened to Vatican II?* London: Sheed & Ward, 1985.

Wolfe, Tom. *The Right Stuff*. New York: Bantam, 1980.

ACKNOWLEDGMENTS

Or rather, the reason why I cannot make acknowledgments. Many hundreds of people have helped me in my travels around the world to gather the material for this book. After having read it, however, the reader will understand that there are many dioceses I must not identify, and many priests, both inside and outside the clerical state, who have begged to remain anonymous. By thanking people by name I risk giving clues for identifying dioceses and individuals.

So to those who received me into their homes with such love, to those who opened their hearts to me, and let me see their tears and their laughter, you have my deepest gratitude, and the gratitude of anyone whom this book may help. May God reward you.

There are, however, two people whom I do want to name. One is Dr. Terry Dosh, executive secretary of Corpus. When I was researching this book he organized the U.S. part of my trip with extraordinary thoroughness. The book owes so very much to Terry and the Corpus members who met me at airports, hosted me, arranged interviews, and shared their lives with me. Terry then scrutinized each chapter after I wrote it, and his suggestions tightened and improved them considerably. My thanks also to my neighbor, writer Gordon Thomas, who, even when ill, took time to show me how to write the proposal for this book. He also suggested the title.

INDEX